HISTORY, PEOPLE AND PLACES

in

NORMANDY

Manor of Pierre Corneille, near Rouen

History, People and Places

in

NORMANDY

BARBARA WHELPTON

SPURBOOKS LIMITED

Published by

SPURBOOKS LTD.

1 Station Road
Bourne End
Buckinghamshire

I S B N   0 902875 57 4

Printed in Great Britain by Compton Printing Ltd.
Aylesbury.

Contents

ILLUSTRATIONS

ACKNOWLEDGEMENTS

The author and the publishers would like to acknowledge the assistance of the French Tourist Offices in London and Normandy, for their assistance in providing photographs for this book.

Other photographs are by R. H. Neillands, and the maps are by Terry Brown.

CHAPTER I

The Face of Normandy

If you look at a map of France, the first noticeable impression of
Normandy is of the Cotentin Peninsula jutting out into the sea like a
clenched fist with the Nez de Jobourg forefinger pointing symbolically
towards America. Though it is not an administrative unit, the Cotentin
stands apart geographically and, to a certain extent, geologically. Since
it has no defined boundaries, all that can be established is that it lies
approximately to the north of a line stretching from Bayeux to Mont
St Michel, which is claimed by both Normandy and Brittany. However
a royal abbey could not be said to belong to either province though, in
fact, it is just within the Norman boundary.

The northern shore of the province, along the Calvados coast, is flat
and sandy, and it was for this reason that it was chosen for the landing
of the Anglo-American forces that invaded Europe on D-Day, the 6th
of June 1944.

A beach on the Calvados coast

The landings on the North coast were held up for a while, by rough seas that are unusual in the summer but do make the development of deep water ports difficult along this shallow coast.

On the other side of the Cotentin the shores of western Normandy are so shallow that in some places the tide recedes for several miles, as for instance at Mont St Michel, where the entire bay empties in the spring, and in the autumn when the sea retreats for nine miles.

On the northern face of the Cotentin there is deep water close to the shore, but prevailing winds and tides are such that the harbour of Cherbourg is mainly artificial in spite of its situation, in what seems, at first sight, to be a sheltered bay.

Incidentally, the countryside in this area is not typical of Normandy —the soil is less fertile, the vegetation less lush, the fields are surrounded by stone walls and rocks appear to be scattered everywhere, though, in regions close to the Gulf Stream, tropical shrubberies abound. This is the area of the 'bocage'.

Forty miles further south it is a different matter: the trees grow with great splendour, the rich pasturages are responsible for the cream, the butter and the cheeses which are celebrated throughout the world. So, for instance, certain Paris restaurant owners insist on buying their

Mont St. Michel

Entrance to Cherbourg harbour

butter at Isigny, a small town noted for its dairy products, and especially cream and cream cheese. Further south still are made the soft and rather pungent cheeses such as Camembert, Pont l'Evêque and the still stronger Livarot. Indeed cream, butter, cider and fish are the basis of Norman gastronomy, but each region claims to have its own special recipes, though the dishes seem to be much the same. Chicken Cauchois, or Chicken à la Vallée d'Auge are cooked in cream and Calvados (apple brandy) and other minor ingredients. The *Sole Dieppoise* also has a cream sauce with mussels, shrimps and mushrooms on a basis of white wine or cider, but many of the other coastal towns boast of a variant of this recipe. Another popular Norman dish is the Tripe à la Mode de Caen, tripe with boned calves foot braised in cider and Calvados, but here again the inns of the inland town of La Ferté-Macé claim to prepare tripe with more or less the same ingredients and even greater succulence.

Good fresh fish and many variants of seafood figure on the menus of inns in all parts of Normandy, but wild duck and tame duck are the speciality of Rouen and the estuary of the Seine. Cider on draught, or

11

A farm at Pont L'Evêque

bottled (cidre bouché) is produced in all parts of Normandy, but is out of favour as a beverage in restaurants since dentists have declared that it is bad for the teeth and the Normans tend to drink Muscadet from nearby Brittany and the Loire. The best fruit comes from the region of Honfleur, but in some places in the Cotentin, where the climate is even milder, figs are grown in the open, as well as mimosa, which blossoms as fully in Normandy as on the Riviera.

The fact is that the mild climate, the fertile soil and the natural intelligence and industry of the population have all contributed to make Normandy a prosperous and happy land from earliest times. The serfs were emancipated soon after the Conquest of England and contented peasants could live in relative comfort, in spite of feudal dues and the outrageous salt tax, as can be seen from the picturesque farmsteads that still remain. Towns such as Rouen, Caen, Alençon and Evreux were given their charters and profited by their liberty to create further prosperity and this is evident from their ancient, if now res-

A view of Rouen, an ancient Norman town

tored, mansions and civic buildings.

The nature of the countryside in Western Europe has been modified and one might almost say created, by the inhabitants. Like the people of Southern England, the Normans tend to surround their fields with hedges, to subsist on a mixed cultivation of pasture, orchards and arable land. They have always cherished and developed their forests, so that there was no shortage of woods for shipbuilding or the construction of half-timbered houses, and they were able to quarry excellent stone for the erection of churches, fortresses and town mansions.

Fortunately only a few of the Abbeys scattered about the countryside of Lower Normandy were damaged beyond repair in the late War and it has been possible to restore them, though the work of restoration is still far from completed. From earliest times, church lands and monastic estates were better and more humanely administered than those of the feudal lords. This is easily apparent, even in the present day, for the countryside near abbeys such as La Trappe and Bec Hélouin has obviously been splendidly cultivated for centuries, and the cottages in the nearby villages testify to centuries of prosperity.

Whilst the majestic Seine which makes Rouen the fourth port in France divides Normandy into two unequal parts, there are besides, numerous little rivers that flow gently through meadows and forests on their way to the sea or to the Seine. Carefully tended, for they need care, they add to the picturesqueness of many a town or village. Of these only the Orne is navigable, and that for a mere fifteen miles. In

A cargo ship on the Seine near Rouen

Southern Normandy, the Sarthe and the Mayenne are largish streams that swell into rivers beyond the boundaries of the province on their way to the Loire.

Incidentally, Southern Normandy is a region of superb forests that appear for a distance of many kilometres between Mortain and Verneuil, in the intervals between a string of the *bastides,* or fortress cities, built by the early Plantagenents. The primeval forests were most probably left intact to stem possible invasions from the Kingdom of France, and for hunting, the chief recreation of medieval kings. Later, castles and splendid châteaux were built in the depths of these sylvan lands, which are still tinged, in places, with the atmosphere of feudalism. The forests themselves are a remnant of those that covered France in Druidical times; splendidly maintained, they are notable for the great variety of trees and the countless ponds and meres that are scattered over the whole of this area. Forests such as these are also to be found in Upper Normandy, but seldom further than thirty miles to the north of the Seine. Still further north they reappear near the boundaries of the province, in a region that is no longer Norman in character: there are few half-timbered houses, the villages have less charm, the inhabitants speak slowly with a dull heavy accent, in contrast to the rather cheerful nasal strains of the other Normans. However, splendid cliffs succeed each other along the coast, and south-west of Dieppe the forests reappear, villages of half-timbered houses nestle among the apple orchards and pasturages surrounded by hedges of hawthorn and may. Cows graze in every meadow, and cows, goats, ducks and pigs throng the farmyards. Living in such surroundings, the Normans are understandably placid, kindly and contented. They are the people of the middle way, unwilling to share in the excesses of Revolution and Civil War, seldom cruel, but easily given to drunkenness and gluttony or shall I say, simply that they have a taste for good food. Nevertheless many Norman peasants begin the day with a tumbler of home distilled Calvados, although distilling is theoretically restricted.

Enjoying, as they do, the fruits of the generous earth, they are at the same time, thrifty and free with their hospitality, eager for gain and yet contented. There is and always has been less poverty in Normandy than anywhere else in France, except perhaps for Touraine. The sea has also provided its bounty, diligently exploited by the immense fishing fleets of Fécamp, Dieppe, and the smaller ports of the Cotentin. Then finally, the estuary of the Seine provides one of the best commercial ports in the world. The combined trade of Rouen, Le Havre and Caen

15

Woods near Mortain

16

is far greater than that of Marseilles which is, taken by itself, the largest port in France, and, indeed, one of the largest ports in the world. The seafaring Normans are still as bold as their Viking ancestors. Several of the pioneers of aviation came from Le Havre whilst yachtsmen from Le Havre or Cherbourg always figure well in ocean contests.

On the map, the Seine is shaped like a cornucopia and, like a cornucopia, it has lavished wealth upon the Normans. Unlike the peasants and countryfolk, the seafarers and merchants have always been prepared to take risks, but it is the inland inhabitants who have been the most creative, except of course for the painters, who have flocked to Normandy, to live and work.

Normandy has the texture of literature because the Norman way of life is varied, interesting and far from superficial. Flaubert and Corneille came from Rouen, but Flaubert, like de Maupassant, his pupil, was at his best when writing about the rustic scene. Culturally endowed towns, such as Honfleur, Dieppe and Le Havre have a remarkable record because they were prosperous, cosmopolitan and at the same time traditional in the best sense of the word. However the inland towns such as Alençon, Verneuil, Dreux and Valognes have also produced a great number of scholars, writers, painters and lawyers of note. To his credit William the Conqueror encouraged the study of law and the building of splendid churches, thus enriching the lives of the Normans for succeeding generations. The Normans are what they are, because of their natural intelligence, common sense and industry, but their character has been influenced by their environment, an environment which was to a large extent shaped by them.

To the visitor, the chief attraction of the province is the immense variety of scenery, from for example the flat beaches of the Cotentin and the Calvados coast, to the rolling hills of the 'Swiss Normand' around Mortain. Normandy is a land of castles, rivers, deep pastures, the close fields of the *bocage,* ancient towns, like Caen, quaint ports like Honfleur, modern spas like Bagnoles, a land full of variety, good food, and history.

CHAPTER II

The Epic of Normandy

In 1911 the Normans celebrated the thousandth anniversary of the Treaty of St Clair-sur-Epte, when Rollo, the Viking, became the first Duke of Normandy, a period covering centuries of adventure, achievement and creativeness. Scarcely a century passed after their establishment in France before Norman adventurers conquered Southern Italy and Sicily. A few years later William Duke of Normandy, crossed the Channel and made himself King of England. The Normans and their kinsmen made their presence felt in every part of Europe. They fought the Moslems in Spain; only the untimely death of the Conqueror prevented him from annexing Wales and Ireland; other Normans took a leading part in the Crusades. In the second half of the 12th century Henry II, King of England and Duke of Normandy, ruled over a Kingdom that stretched from the boundaries of Scotland to the Pyrenees, a realm that included two thirds of France and was richer and more powerful than the Holy Roman Empire. His son, John Lackland, allowed Normandy to be taken from him by King Philip Augustus, together with many other rich domains of the Angevin Empire, and Normandy became a province of France, but the Normans continued to be as bold and as adventurous as ever. They lost none of the supreme qualities which have blazoned their name in so many parts of the world, and helped them to tide over so many vicissitudes including their greatest trial of all, during the hostilities of the Second World War.

Normandy, as we shall see, is a land of rich pasture, slow flowing rivers, and splendid forests, producing the finest cattle and sheep in France. Until recently the seas that wash its shores were full of all kinds of fish. Scarcely, it would seem, the country in which bold adventurers would settle and keep their spirit of adventure, but Rollo the Viking knew what he was about when he took over Normandy as a Duchy from the French King, Charles the Simple in 911 A.D. The Normans camped on the right bank of the river while the French remained on

Statue of William the Conqueror at Falaise

the left, and the new province was created in order to stop the Vikings from raiding the other parts of France, as they had done for so many years. Indeed, the name 'Norman' developed from the word 'Northman', the general term for all pirates, Viking or not.

The territory taken over was bounded by the Epte to the north and by the Avre to the south, representing rather less than two thirds of the Normandy of today.

However, there is a French proverb to the effect that the Normans have hooks on their hands (*Les Normands ont la patte croche*) and make a point of acquiring everything within their reach. By the middle of the 10th century the Cotentin, or the Cherbourg Peninsula had been added to the Duchy as well as the lands that lie at its base.

Until the coming of the Northmen, the region that became Normandy was populated, like most of the rest of France, by people of Celtic stock who had acquired their speech and culture from the Romans during the four centuries of their occupation of Gaul. The Teutonic Franks had then conquered Gaul, but were, after many years, absorbed by the Latinised population. Astonishingly, the assimilation of the Normans was far swifter, but this was because they left their women behind them and found wives or concubines among the native population of their new lands. So their children were brought up as Catholics, speaking only French, and without any knowledge of the language and traditions of their paternal ancestors. In many rural districts the Nordic strain appears to be predominant even to the present day. In some regions the villagers are tall, blue-eyed and fair-haired like Swedes, but, throughout Normandy, the racial stock tends to be blue-eyed and brown-haired, as if the blend of Latin and Viking were complete.

The Normans of today, like the Normans in the novels of Flaubert and de Maupassant, tend to be cautious, yet brave and adventurous if circumstances require. They are lavish in their hospitality, apt to drink hard and indulge in gargantuan meals. The celebrations of country weddings still include three or four days of drinking, and eating food that would not be out of place at a Lord Mayor's banquet.

Without being verbose and indulging in the torrential spate of words that characterise the Southern French, the Normans of all classes love good conversation and have a sense of incident which is manifested in the short stories of their best authors.

Like most French people they are contentious and given to indulging in lawsuits at the slightest excuse, as much for the pleasure of legal procedure as from the wish to assert their rights, and to profit from their opponents.

William the Conqueror became the sixth Duke of Normandy in 1035 and, even before the invasion of England, he encouraged the Benedictines to re-establish themselves in the province and to rebuild the numerous abbeys which had been ruined and plundered by the Vikings in past centuries. By great good fortune, he decided to establish a second capital at Caen at a safe distance from the French frontier, near the disputed city of Mantes.

The churches and abbeys of Caen were constructed in the Romanesque tradition and in the beautiful honey-coloured limestone quarried in the neighbourhood, and later exported to England after the Conquest for the erection of castles and churches such as the Tower of London or Canterbury Cathedral in places conveniently situated near a navigable river. Incidentally the Benedictines were used by William as spies to prepare for the Conquest of England during the last years of the life of Edward the Confessor.

Clearly, by the middle of the 11th century, the Normans had ceased to be great seamen, for William had the utmost difficulty in collecting ships to transport his small army across the Channel. Assembling his fleet at Dives, not far from Cabourg, he had to wait weeks for

Memorial to the Conqueror's men at Barfleur

The Modern University at Caen

favourable weather and even then, he could only proceed to St Valéry-sur-Somme on the northern frontier of the Duchy, where he had to wait again before setting out on his great venture.

The Norman contribution to English history is too well known to be set out in detail here. Suffice to say that England was able to enjoy a greater share of European culture from the introduction of French architects, masons, sculptors and stained glass artists, together with the Romanesque style of architecture which soon developed into a style of its own, known in Britain as Norman.

For three centuries French was the language of the Court, of the gentry and of the men of letters. The Anglo-Norman, Thomas, author of the best version of Tristram and Iseult, was one of the most notable exponents of French literature in the Middle Ages.

On the other hand, Norman minstrels began to make use of the Celtic legends of Britain which were developed in France into the Arthurian cycle, translated later on into English by Mallory in the 15th century.

However, William I was not the first Norman to carve out for himself a kingdom overseas, for even before the Conquest three of the Hauteville brothers had stormed and captured town after town in Southern Italy at the head of bands of from fifty to two hundred of their compatriots. Eventually the last surviving member of the three claimed to be King of Sicily, Apulia and Amalfi, and he was succeeded by his son Roger II.

Of Robert Guiscard, the most energetic of the three brothers, Gibbon wrote: 'In less than three years, he enjoyed the glory of delivering a Pope (Gregory VII) from the Holy Roman Emperor, Henry IV, and of compelling the two Emperors of the East and of the West to fly before his victorious arms'. Guiscard died in Greece, and his death put an end to the dream of a Norman making himself Emperor of Byzantium.

As might have been expected, both the Norman, and, later the Angevin Kings of England were constantly at war with the Kings of France. In 1195, Richard I built the mighty Château Gaillard at Les Andelys as a key fortress to stem an invasion of Normandy along the Valley of the Seine by Philip Augustus. It was captured nine years later in the reign of the lamentable King John who was unable to prevent the annexation of Normandy by the French.

Whilst the first invasion of France by the English, in the Hundred Years War had no lasting effects, the conquest of Northern France by Henry V was a different matter. Normandy was reoccupied by the English from 1415 to 1450. Under the beneficent regency of John, Duke of Bedford, the University of Caen was established, and two of the loveliest Gothic churches in Rouen were founded. He died in 1435, fifteen years before the liberation of Normandy by the forces of Charles VII, but his University at Caen, still survives, now modernised and greatly expanded.

When England ceased to be a threat to the autonomy of France, it was only natural that the coastal towns of Normandy should begin to prosper, especially after the discovery of the New World. As early as 1362, adventurers sailed as far as Guinea to found a city there named Dieppe. In the beginning of the 15th century, Jean de Béthencourt discovered the Canary Islands and made himself King of that archipelago.

Then, in turn, seamen from Honfleur, Dieppe and Havre opened up regions of North and South America, including, more especially, Quebec, founded as a Norman colony by Samuel Champlain of Dieppe.

The expansion of trade by sea was all the more remarkable in that Normandy has no good natural harbours. Under the Romans,

23

The harbour basin, Honfleur, home of many Norman seamen

Lillebonne on the Seine flourished but later, when the river silted up in the early Middle Ages, it was replaced first of all by Caen, which had the navigable River Orne, then Harfleur and Honfleur, at the mouth of the estuary of the Seine; and later Dieppe and Fécamp. In 1517, the port of Le Havre was built to replace Harfleur which had ceased to be operative. Time and again efforts were made to use harbours on the north coast, but, as the Allies discovered in 1944, they are too shallow and the prevailing winds and tides make access to these shores difficult in bad weather. Even Cherbourg, first founded as a naval base in the 17th century, has had to have an artificially constructed harbour that only became really practicable with the advent of steam.

In the Franco-Prussian War of 1870-71 the hostilities did not spread to the coastal ports because of the intervention of the British Government, and there were no naval engagements in the Channel. During the First World War, Normandy was untouched, but the destruction wrought in the Second War beggars description. In 1940, the Germans bombed Neufchâtel-en-Bray, Yvetôt, Caudebec and Rouen. In 1944 entire cities were completely destroyed in the course of hostilities, when two million men fought for three months across the province; not only the villages near the landing beaches, but also Caen (pop: 60,000), Le Havre (pop: 180,000), St Lô (15,000) and dozens of small towns and villages besides, as well as the centres of Rouen, Lisieux and many other ancient cities. The port installations of Le Havre were completely destroyed, as well as those of Caen and the factories in its vicinity. In Le Havre alone, 5000 people were killed outright by the Allied bombardments, and of course tens of thousands were rendered homeless throughout the province.

To this, their greatest hour of trial, the Normans reacted magnificently. They decided to rebuild, if possible even better than before. Le Havre was reconstructed in concrete on a new and entirely original, imaginative plan, of great spaciousness. Other places were restored to their previous state with the use of the beautiful and appropriate local stone. Where possible, churches and monuments were repaired and renovated, but also a number of churches and public buildings were constructed in a bold and original manner, employing not only really modern architects, but sculptors and workers in stained glass who succeeded in many cases in blending contemporary trends with the traditional spirit.

The reconstruction of Normandy has been so effective that it is now one of the most prosperous regions in the whole of Europe, and the

25

The new museum at Le Havre

glowing stone gives to the many reconstructed towns, a timeless air, as if they had stood so for centuries, and were not re-established, within the last thirty years, out of the rubble of the Normandy fighting of 1944. Their antiquity may be an illusion, but their charm is a reality.

CHAPTER III

Dieppe and the Environs

'Fair stands the wind for France', and it lies fairest of all for Dieppe, the oldest of the three Norman ports and one still retaining the aura of an old-fashioned sea-side resort combined with the colour and liveliness of a fishing harbour and markets.

The white chalk cliffs which sweep down to the broad beach are almost a replica of the cliffs of Dover, but the vast area of grass which divides the busy Boulevard de Verdun from the sea gives the sea front a spaciousness lacking on the English side of the Channel. The tremendous scope of sky and sea is relieved by the dramatic silhouette of the castle to the east, grimly fortified above the town, but oddly enough becoming almost ethereal when floodlit against an indigo sky at night.

Castle at Dieppe

Within a few minutes of landing, the traveller can be exploring the varied coastline, the woods, the rich pastures, the farmlands, rivers and forests and the villages with their ancient churches and manor houses which lie nearby. Though he will surely wish to stay awhile in Dieppe itself and wander along the gay high street with its good shops and really beautiful houses with their elegant wrought iron balconies and even, here and there, a fascinating old courtyard.

A 19th century atmosphere still prevails and the ghosts of the Impressionists, of Oscar Wilde, of Sickert and Jongkind linger in the old town.

Individual purveyors of mussels and shrimps continue to trundle their barrows through the crowded streets and there is the sharp tang of the sea mingling with the pervading smell of fresh fish, and a general air of expectancy and excitement in the harbour and under the arcades which for some reason is far stronger, in a French port, than anywhere else in the world.

The Café des Tribunaux at the Puits Salé—the social centre of the town—is a cheerful place to sit and watch the animated crowds surging round the fountain from which has flowed since the 16th century the spring waters of Saint Aubin sur Scie. A short stroll away stands the Gothic church of St Jacque with its fine rose window and, even nearer, is the less interesting, partly Renaissance, church of St Remy. It was the church of St Jacques which Camille Pissarro chose to paint during his stay in Dieppe. He depicted the same square in sunlight and in mist; crowded with people when the fair was on or even when it was completely deserted.

For the museum-minded the castle has, in addition to the inevitable local archaeological finds, a good collection of 19th century French and Dutch paintings and a highly interesting and unusual collection of ivory carvings by craftsmen who came to the town in the Middle Ages to work on the ivory brought back from Africa by the mariners of Dieppe. They established flourishing workshops which prospered into the 19th century when the demand for boxes, fans, crucifixes and statuettes intricately worked in increasingly expensive ivory, rapidly decreased.

It was against Dieppe that the 2nd Canadian Division, and British commandos launched 'Operation Jubilee' in 1942. The Dieppe raid was a total failure, but served to provide some valuable lessons for the Normandy landings of 1944. Of the thousands of men who made the assault some two-thirds were killed or taken prisoner, and Dieppe maintains close links with Canada, links forged during the bloody

Les Tourelles, Dieppe

fighting on the beaches of the town.

Whenever I make more than a fleeting visit to Dieppe I drive out westwards and spend an hour or so revisiting the nearby villages where their beautiful Norman churches have some remarkable modern stained glass. Were they not so crowded in the season, the coastal resorts are delightful to stay in and most of them have beaches set against steep chalk cliffs, or occupy a picturesque bay swept clean by a strong tide.

The road westwards twists up and down along the coast to Pourville through pleasant country to turn inland and steeply uphill for Varengeville, where the houses are scattered along the embankments of the road, and farms have picture-book farmyards with great horses, pigs and chickens and a shaggy donkey usually loudly braying. The church at Varengeville on the edge of the cliff is wonderfully sited, and dates from the 12th and 14th centuries retaining many Romanesque features. The deeply glowing stained glass window of the Tree of Jesse is by Georges Braque who is buried in the churchyard. It was this artist also who designed the small window in sea-wave colours in the chapel of St Dominique nearby.

Georges Braque was born in Argenteuil in 1882, the son of an amateur artist. The family went to Paris when Georges was still a child,

Cliffs and beaches near Dieppe

and he was still young when they settled in Le Havre, a region to which the artist frequently returned to paint when he was working in Paris at his studio in Montmartre. He was very much influenced by Cézanne and was, for a time, associated with the Fauves and then, developing the Cubist principles explored by Cézanne, he became a leader with Picasso of the Cubist movement.

His painting was interrupted by the First World War when he was wounded in 1915 and commended for bravery. Everyone is familiar with his monumentally designed still lifes with his subtle though robustly earthy colours vibrant with light, but perhaps the greatest of all his works are to be found amongst his sea and beach studies of grounded boats, of cliffs and fishing huts, where his mastery of spatial relationships and exquisite command of colour, are so apparent.

For historians and architects, the great interest of Varengeville lies in the Manor House of Ango which stands a little inland. Though considerably restored it is a fine example of a seignorial dwelling; it was built in the 16th century by a rich shipowner from Dieppe who was banker to Francis I and nicknamed the Medici of Dieppe. The building is arranged round a square with the tower at one corner from which he was able to look down upon the movement of ships in the port of Dieppe, bringing back immense quantities of merchandise and the ivory to be carved in the workshops of Dieppe. Medallions on the façade represent Francis I and Diane de Poitiers who were frequent guests there. The house is constructed in black flint and white stone arranged in mosaic patterns; in the centre stands the vast round tower or dovecote with intricately designed stone and brick facings.

Whilst he was living in this mansion, Ango frequently lent the King large sums of money and even a fleet, but he was ruined by jealous cabals after his death.

Returning inland from the church of Varengeville the main road passes through pleasant pastoral country to Ste Marguerite which is surrounded by woods. Beyond lies an enchanting seashore under the cliffs—enchanting, that is to the eye, but not a superb bathing beach. This delightful village possesses one of the most lovely small Romanesque churches in Normandy; it is set back in a graveyard on a slight eminence. As we enter through the Romanesque portal with its carved capitals, we feel the atmosphere of warm, mellow stone, of simple perfection, yet with enough variety of detail to be worthy of close study. One twisted pillar has shell and sea motifs decorating the fluting. The 12th century altar is very plain, but when this is decorated with deep red roses, and swallows are darting low beneath the beamed roof, the images created by the masons, the warm tones of the stonework and the general atmosphere of a much loved village church is enhanced. Max Ingrand was responsible for the modern glass windows which are to my mind a little harsh in colour and startling in effect in this tranquil setting, though this considerable artist has produced some very beautiful windows including those we shall see later at Yvetot.

Just outside the church on the wall of the Mairie a tablet to the Allied commandos tells us that:—

'On the 19th August 1942 the disembarkation of Allied Commandos under the orders of Lord Lovat took place. After having destroyed the enemy batteries of Blancmesnil, these glorious soldiers re-embarked at Vasterval.'

These villages lie in a countryside verdant and lush, so lush I have been told by local farmers that it is too damp for sheep; this would account for the preponderance of cattle in the region.

The road to Bourg Dun is a dull one, but the church is worth a visit by devotees of church architecture as it is almost like a Renaissance Château with its entrance portal and turret and it contains a very lovely font of the 16th century with bas-relief panels. The general effect of the interior is lofty and light, but the stained glass windows are totally inferior to the rest of the building.

Back on the coast, the charming seaside resort of Veules-les-Roses, is quite as attractive as its name—the beach is reached through a cutting in the chalk cliffs, like many along this coast. The coast and hinterland beyond this point will be described in a later chapter, but there are other places of interest inland in close proximity to Dieppe.

A road south-east runs through the Valley of Arques to Arques-la-Bataille. This small industrial town runs steeply uphill to the ruins of the feudal castle which commands magnifient views. An obelisk on a knoll on the other side of the river commemorates the victory of Henry IV with his 7,000 men over the 30,000 strong army of the Catholic League led by the Duke of Mayenne in 1589.

The Church of Notre Dame was completed in 1515 and has a very beautiful rood screen in stone with fluted columns, which was added in the 17th century.

The small area east of Arques has all that is left of the Forest of Arques—a very ancient forest which once stretched for miles over this region.

CHAPTER IV

Eu to Lyon-le-Forêt

If we begin our exploration of Normandy by taking the coast road to the east of Dieppe we shall pass through Puys, now a suburb of the port. It lies beyond the Cité des Limes once thought to be Caesar's camp, but in fact a far more ancient site, later occupied by the Gauls, the Romans and the Norsemen. Then comes Berneval also a rather dull suburb with only the memory of the valiant parachute raid in the early days of the war to distinguish it from neighbouring resorts. The coast road itself is attractive enough but can be misty and mournful so it is better to dip down to the parallel inland route to St Martin en Campagne, set in pastoral countryside with, beyond it, a delightful manor house surrounded by woods. The road is bordered with fine groups of trees and wide fields where splendid cattle graze, regular rows of trees act as wind breaks and farmhouses are further protected by being set in orchards; then the landscape gradually becomes more intimate towards Tocqueville with the gentler lines of poplars and small farms.

At Tocqueville a road swings inland to Eu, a quiet little town between the sea and the splendid forest of the same name; the château has been constantly restored and architecturally has little claim to distinction. Nevertheless the dusky brown and pink of the brickwork, the pale honey of the facings and the variety of the roofline of silvery grey is pleasing enough to the eye and the setting is truly superb. Here is an example of a large building, and its beautifully designed gardens and park with the unmistakable genius of Le Nôtre, complementing and being part of the countryside which creeps up to it on all sides. Magnificent chestnuts in bloom must enhance the aspect in late spring and the imposing entrance gates in front of the château with a smaller one with little lions to the left make a fascinating ensemble.

Since there is a surfeit of châteaux—and churches—in Normandy there is little point in visiting them all and many of them decorate the landscape with inspired architecture, but can be repetitive in the

Louis-Phillipe's Chateau at Eu

interior. I think that Eu is one that can be missed from the point of view of the interior except by the most ardent of sightseers. On the other hand it houses mementoes of the Orleans family, and the history of this family is of especial interest to the British.

The town originally belonged to the Dukes of Normandy and passed through the hands of the Nevers, the Guise, Mlle de Montpensier and the Duke of Maine and then the Orleans family who owned the Château until it became the town museum. It is famous as the place where William the Conqueror received Harold, and where he married his Flemish wife. There is also a legend that Joan of Arc was imprisoned here, but there is no historical record of this event.

Louis Philippe was descended from Philippe of Orleans, brother of Louis XIV and therefore of Bourbon stock. It was on these grounds that Talleyrand was able to manoeuvre the French to elect this prince King of the French after the people of Paris had rebelled against the autocratic Charles X and forced him to take refuge in England.

Of portly figure, and of middle class ways, the new king was supported at first by the French bourgeoisie during the first years of his reign (1830-1848), though eventually he was driven out like his predecessor because he also refused to extend the franchise and tried to introduce a form of censorship.

Once again the populace of the capital rose against their sovereign, who had to flee with less decorum than Charles X, for he had to escape from the Tuileries with the Queen and, heavily disguised, they found shelter first of all in a gardener's cottage at Honfleur but were eventually smuggled to Newhaven, by the British consul at Havre, as Mr and Mrs Smith. Eventually they settled at Claremont in Surrey, taking the titles of Count and Countess de Neuilly.

Born in 1773, he had followed the example of his father, Philippe l'Egalité and became such an ardent supporter of the Revolution that he joined the Jacobin Club in 1790, and by 1792, at the age of eighteen, he became a lieutenant-general taking part with some success in the victories of Valmy and Jemappes. The following year he realised that he might become a victim of the terror and so he fled to Germany and after some years of wandering he settled in Twickenham and remained there until 1807 when he went to Sicily, where he married the daughter of the King of Naples. In order to make full provision for the house that he bought in Palermo he had sent to him from England twenty-two water closets, and twenty-four English housemaids. As far as I know, no-one has discovered the ultimate fate of these young women, though it seems probable that some of them may have married Sicilians and that perhaps they have among their descendants prominent members of the *mafia*.

In 1815 Louis Philippe returned to France, and most of his vast estates, including those in the region of Eu, were restored to him by order of King Louis XVIII. It was at this juncture that the Duke of Orleans, as he was then, ordered the palace to be restored, and it soon became his favourite place of residence. Later, when he became King of the French, Louis Philippe set out to gain the support of England since his accession to the throne by means of the Revolution of 1830 aroused the hostility of autocratic nations such as Prussia, Austria and Russia. His knowledge of English and of the English facilitated the cementing of this *entente* and Queen Victoria and Prince Albert twice accepted his hospitality at Eu.

Both Prince Albert and the Queen were enchanted with the palace as it was then, for part of it was destroyed by fire in 1902.

'The people of Eu,' noted the Queen in her journal, 'were different from the English.' Nevertheless she and her husband established most cordial relations with Louis Philippe and Queen Amélie and the friendship continued after the exile of the French sovereigns in England. Unlike Napoleon III, his successor, she considered Louis-

Philippe was thoroughly French in character, 'possessing all the liveliness and talkativeness of that people.'

She also commented upon his vast knowledge upon all and every subject and his great activity of mind. She wrote in glowing terms to her uncle of her reception at Eu:

'I write to you from this dear place, where we are in the midst of this admirable and truly amiable family, and where we feel quite at home and as if we were one of them. Our reception by the dear King and Queen has been most kind, and by the people really gratifying.'

A note was added here that the Queen was enthusiastically received at Le Tréport, a flourishing fishing port and bathing resort nearby, where a great entertainment was given in the banqueting-room of the Château and, two days later, a *fête champêtre* on the Mont d'Orléans in the forest.

A most impressive equestrian statue of Louis Philippe is set against trees to the left of the Château.

The Collegiate church of Notre Dame and St Lawrence is quite another matter. Lawrence O'Toole, Primate of Ireland, died in Eu in the 12th century and the Cathedral was built in the early Gothic style of the 12th and 13th century. Even though Viollet-le-Duc carried out a rather unimaginative restoration of the building, it is still a fine example of Early Norman Gothic and the interior is not only remarkable for its spaciousness and beautiful proportions but also contains some very lovely sculpture including a splendid 15th century *Entombment* and a *Head of Christ,* a statue of Our Lady of Eu and a wooden relief of the Nativity. Most impressive of all is a recumbent figure of St Lawrence in the restored Crypt, carved in the 12th or 13th

Statue of Louis-Philippe at Eu

The College Chapel at Eu

century and lying amongst figures of the Artois family.

The College Chapel, only a few steps from the church, has a really beautiful Renaissance façade in soft pink brick with a majestic door-way surmounted by two more storeys and a gracefully curved pediment, the whole flanked by two towers with violet grey cupolas. The College was founded in 1573 by Henri de Guise and the Chapel built in 1620 by his widow, Catherine of Cleves. It contains a fine 17th century marble mausoleum of the Duke who was assassinated by the orders of Henry III of France in 1588.

A broad strip of beautiful forest land runs south-east from Eu stretching as far as Blagny-sur-Bresle, a town almost totally destroyed in the Second World War. This once enormous forest is still very large and affords the most lovely drives, or better still, walks. It is a region to wander and get lost in, to explore the small narrow roads and forest avenues, to come across an attractive hamlet or an old church or manor house framed by its setting of trees. Those who like curiosities should search for the Bonne Entente, a few yards off the D278. This is the name given to a beech and an oak which have developed so close together that they seem like one tree bearing both oak and beech leaves.

Beyond Blagny you can leave the Upper Forest of Eu and continue through the rich pasturelands along the valley of the Bresle to Aumale, a small milk marketing town on the eastern frontier of Normandy which only retains vestiges of its historic past. One of the Counts of Aumale fought at the Battle of Hastings and his English descendants were the Albemarle family. The town was many times besieged, notably by William Rufus and Charles the Bold. Henry IV was defeated and badly wounded here fighting against the Spaniards. The main monument of the town is a Renaissance church with 16th century glass.

From here a network of small roads runs through peaceful countryside to Neufchâtel-en-Bray. This is a long way round and there are direct main roads from Blagny and Aumale for those who prefer them, but Normandy is a region where travelling from one point to another is often more enjoyable than the arrival, and though perhaps not so romantic nor so spectacular as other parts of Normandy it has the intimate charm of tranquil streams and pastures and hamlets without any popular monumental points to attract crowds of sightseers.

Neufchâtel-en-Bray is of course the centre from which are sold the delicious Neufchâtel cheeses—bondons—made in the farmhouses of the surrounding countryside. Perhaps it is no longer true that as Palgrave wrote: 'You smell the cheese in every room of your inn', but the region is still 'the dairy of Paris'.

Since it is not necessary to go to Neufchâtel to sample these cheeses its greatest interest for me lies in the splendid rebuilding of the civic centre and the restoration of the Church of Nôtre Dame which is not yet completed, but it still retains its badly damaged 15th century door, the 13th-century chancel and 16th century nave. The original 12th century transept was reconstructed in the 19th century.

In the civic centre the round theatre is built of reddish brick with deep blue lights in a spacious setting of lawns and on the other side of the main street, a sloping lawn planted with glowing deep red Frensham roses sweeps to the Palais de Justice with a huge sculpture head of concrete set on a terrace. The rest of the modern town is spaciously planned and built of silvery grey stone. The attractive streets of what remains of the old town have been tidied up but are still picturesque with their little gardens.

One great advantage of staying in Neufchâtel-en-Bray is the number of walks or short excursions which can be taken in this dairy farming region which has recently also increased its production of apples, both dessert and cider, so that in spring there is the added attraction of acres of blossoming orchards and, in late summer and autumn, the trees are almost as brilliant with bright red fruit.

This undulating green countryside which the French describe so graphically as 'accidenté' in the middle of the rather bare Caux plateau, is the result of a movement of the earth's crust which formed the Alps, and its repercussions raised ridges across France. One of these developed a lopsided dome of land with a steep north-eastern slope now split and hollowed out by continuous erosions. From this depression, known as the Bray buttonhole, flow the rivers Epte and Andelle, and only a few miles away, the rivers Béthune, Terrain and Varenne make the whole area into a watershed.

A winding road north out of Neufchâtel (N314) leads past the bare north-eastern slope and a turning left towards the Forêt du Hellet gives wide views of the Béthune Valley and continues right across the forest to Croixdalle; a curve left turns left again through Osmay St Valéry and over a rise into the next valley. Small roads running south-east from here, lead to Bully and Neufchâtel. However, anyone not returning to Neufchâtel but still working south, would do better to follow the Valley of the Béthune along the main road to Mesnières-en-Bray from which, of course, it is also only a few miles back to Neufchâtel.

Mesnières-en-Bray is chiefly remarkable for its Château built in the Renaissance style and very much more beautiful than the one at Eu, being totally satisfying in design, proportion and colour which is creamy white and silver grey. This restraint is enhanced by the effect of the masses of red geraniums along the green lawns.

The Château is really composed of a central portion with a steep sloping roof and arcading flanked by towers with two wings at right angles ending in large round towers with conical roofs. This entrance was originally by a drawbridge but replaced by a monumental stairway in the 18th century rising over a stone bridge and leading into the courtyard. The whole is in a charming rural setting and surrounded by a wall of compressed white chalk with small towers with grey shingle roofs. The Château is now an ecclesiastical college, the Institute of St. Joseph, and can only be visited by special arrangement on Sundays but there is an excellent view of it from the main gateway and there are no coaches, no cars or tourists, in fact it is utterly peaceful even in summer.

Strangely enough, the church in the village is incredibly ugly in a curious chequered assortment of pink brick.

The main road from Neufchâtel to Forges-les-Eaux lies through very open and not very exciting country. The side roads to the west, though

39

not very easy to follow, are far more attractive and go through some wooded countryside.

Forges-les-Eaux is beautifully laid out and gay with flowered balconies. It is a charmingly situated watering place which was very fashionable in the reigns of Louis XIII and Louis XIV and it was here that Mlle de Montpensier, La Grande Mademoiselle, was apt to come for a cure. There is a grotto in the park where Louis XIII and his wife Anne of Austria and Richelieu took the waters.

There still remain some delightful old buildings and in particular a little square of picturesque half-timbered houses made even more attractive by varying subtle colourwashes. Just beyond the spa on the road to Lyons-la-Forêt, there is the most enchanting fairytale château on the right, pink and cream and silver, very small and turretted and spired.

There is a highroad from Forges to Gournay-en-Bray but it is pleasanter to take a longer route south to Argueil then across country east to Gournay. Argueil is a delightful little village with a 16th century church with an excessively and proudly tall spire, a landmark for miles. The byroads are lined with farms amongst orchards and the aspect is extremely rural, but has great character. It is a basic sculptured kind of land with dryer, less lush uplands where sheep graze, and fields of golden stubble in September.

A lovely country road runs south-east from Argueil to Gournay-en-Bray—a town with an ancient church of St Hildeverts, but perhaps better known for its Petit Suisse cheese, the result of a farmer's wife being helped by a Swiss cowherd to mix fresh curds with cream.

The river, the Epte, has formed the western frontier of Normandy since the 10th century.

A good highway leads directly along the valley to Gisors but the secondary roads on the other side of the river are much more attractive and may well lure you westwards before you reach your goal.

Gisors was very badly damaged in the Second World War, but the ancient fortress still dominates the town and contrasts with the charm of the lower-edged waters of the Epte which flows through the town. The church comprises a number of different styles from the 13th century onwards, although foundations of a much earlier date have been discovered during the course of restoration.

There is a beautiful patch of country along the valley of the Epte which continues to run southwards but veering to the west. Here the river flows between gently undulating hills with softly outlined trees along the skyline. An abundance of wild flowers bloom in the

The Chateau at Gisors

hedgerows, and avenues of poplars make their familiar mistletoe-decked silhouette against the wide sky.

It was here at St Clair-sur-Epte that the Duchy of Normandy was created by Rollo, and Charles the Simple. According to Dudon St Quentin, the first chronicler of Normandy, the two men clasped hands and the duchy of Normandy came into being, the Epte and the Avre being the duchy's boundaries to the north and south of the Seine in the terms of the Agreement. Rollo was betrothed to the king's daughter, and became a Christian.

St Clair was martyred in 811 near the present Hermitage where pilgrims come to bath their eyes in the waters of the fountain. The rather unattractive church was built mainly in the 12th and 15th century and has a gentle 13th century Virgin above the portal. It keeps vestiges of its Carolingian past.

Further south and just before the town of Vernon and the Seine lies Giveray in its peaceful setting of tall poplars, willows and lush meadows.

This is the village where Claude Monet lived in his later years. When after the terrible struggle of his early days he at last became successful at the age of 50, he bought the house on the Gisors road and extended the 'miserable orchard' and elaborated the garden which he spent so much time painting. He even diverted some of the waters of the Epte to construct his famous lily pond. He painted it again and again with the lilies in bud, with the lilies full open, in sunshine, in mist, at sunset. When he was 76 years old, he built a second garden studio and began work on the series of the Nymphéas and it was to this studio that Clémenceau came to choose the paintings for the State.

Monet could see very little towards the end of his life and was blind in one eye, but mercifully he did not become totally blind until a few days before his death in 1926.

A deep nostalgia hangs over the beautiful garden which can be seen from the road. The fragile little Japanese bridge still crosses the lily pond and the branches of willows brush the rippling waters and scatter shadows over the flowers. Whilst on the other side of the road, roses climb up the pergolas to the front door of his house and the country flowers and fruit trees he loved so much flourish in the front garden.

From the bridge at Vernon there is a far reaching view of the Seine and its wooded islands and there are some attractive 15th century houses near the collegiate church of Notre Dame founded in the 12th century and completed in the 15th with later modifications. A fine rose window on the west front is flanked by two elegant soaring spires supported by flying buttresses. Remains of fortifications built by the Angevin Kings of England still stand on both banks of the river. The Tour des Archives was the keep of the 12th century castle, and the Château des Tourelles, on the opposite bank at Veronet was built by Edward I. It formed part of the defences of the old bridge and can be seen amongst the trees.

The Forests of Vernon and of Andelys fill in the curve of the Seine to Les Andelys where the dramatic Château Gaillard is set majestically on the steep cliffs of one of the most beautiful settings on the river. This was Richard Lionheart's fortress, Richard, King of England and Duke of Normandy, who had it constructed in 1196 to prevent the French King, Philip Augustus, from reaching Rouen along the Seine Valley. He succeeded in this object, but when John Lackland became king, the French hoped to starve the defenders into surrender. On learning that they could withstand isolation for many months, Philip Augustus decided to storm it. By partly filling in the very deep moat and mining one of the towers the French succeeded in forcing a way through the outer stronghold and entering the main defences, pulling down the drawbridge and finally forcing the garrison to surrender.

Even those who are not interested in the remains of castles will find it worth while to climb or drive up behind the castle for the splendid view of Les Andelys and the lovely sweep of the Seine. The castle itself comprises a Redoubt and a main fort separated by a deep moat, it once had five towers of which only one subsists and a main fort separated from the redoubt by a moat. This is now crossed by a footbridge which gives access to the keep with its enormously thick walls. Originally it had three storeys each approached by wooden ladders which could quickly be pulled up.

Les Andelys is really two villages—Grand and Petit—lying about a mile apart. Petit Andely is dominated by the castle, and has the Gothic Church of St Saviour with a 14th century wooden porch, but Grand Andely has Notre Dame, Gothic and Renaissance in style with a fine Renaissance organ and loft and some good 16th century stained glass.

It was at Villers, to the east of Les Andelys, that Nicolas Poussin the painter was born in 1594, so he was a true Norman, although only his early years were spent in Normandy where as a young boy he received some instruction from a painter from Beauvais; he continued his training in Paris when he was 18. At 30 he went to Rome and it was here that he found his deepest inspiration and was influenced by the antique and by the paintings and drawings of Raphael. Like many classical painters, he studied his effects by means of a model stage with wax figures and experimental lighting. His fame as a painter of figure compositions illustrating dramatic events became such that he was called back to the French Court to paint for King Louis XIII and Cardinal Richelieu in 1640. Despite his high position and the esteem in which he was held, he was unhappy in France and, after less than two years, he contrived to go back to Rome where he worked until he died in 1665. Some of his figure compositions in landscape setting show the influence of his native Normandy in their pastoral calm, and the play of light on splendid trees.

From Les Andelys a beautiful narrow road runs north-east to Ecouis which has an old collegiate church built in the 13th and 14th century by Enguerrand de Marighy, Superintendent of Finances to Philip the Fair. The exterior is disappointing, mainly due to 18th century reconstruction, but inside there is a most remarkable collection of sculpture commissioned by the Finance Minister. The most famous is St Mary the Egyptian, more generally called Our Lady of Ecouis, a ravishingly beautiful, sinuous figure with rippling hair and draperies flowing in perfect harmony.

The road continues northwards through the Forêt de Lyons covering undulating country with beautiful slender trees rising gracefully amongst splendid oaks, never dark or gloomy in atmosphere, but with a tracery of light flooding through the branches and patterning the ground. It was one of the favourite hunting grounds of the Dukes of Normandy. It has the delightful magical atmosphere well fitted as a setting to the little town of Lyons-la-Forêt.

Now basically Lyons-la-Forêt is a most beautiful small town of half-timbered houses, but it has been a little over-restored, a little too well kept up and seems almost too good to be true. Even so, it is a delightful place in an historic forest which needs exploring in depth to see Menesqueville with its 12th century church and very old statues and the Abbey of Mortemer with its 12th and 13th century ruins of a Cistercian abbey. The Forest also has a number of ancient and enormous oaks and beeches singled out for special attention by signposts.

Out of season and freed from the carloads of trippers which come to marvel at its tranquil streets lined by colourwashed and half-timbered houses and beautifully tended gardens, the town itself has much to recommend it. The old market is protected by a splendid 18th century timber roof and the 15th century church has a timber belfry and fine wooden statues. The Hôtel de Ville is of Louis XIV architecture and there are a number of lovely old 15th century manor houses. The Hôtel de la Licorne is a lovely old inn in the place du Marché and dates from the early 17th century. It has a Louis XIII staircase. Added to all this it serves excellent regional food.

North-westwards through the forest lies the Château of Vascoeuil which has been to some extent reconstructed to give a typical Norman setting of half-timbered cottages, a park with landscaped gardens and flowing water flanked by flower beds. It is the kind of legendary Château in soft dusky rose and cream with a turret and mellowed walls dreamed of in childhood and almost too perfect to have much impact on the sophisticated. From time to time exhibitions of great interest such as modern works by Salvator Dali and modern Aubusson tapestries are held there.

North-eastwards through intricate roads along which it is quite acceptable to get lost, lies Clères, almost directly north of Rouen, with a fascinating zoo which mainly specialises in birds: storks, peacocks, pink flamingoes, duck and oriental geese and numerous species of waterbirds, as well as aviaries of tropical birds. In the inner reserve, antelope, kangaroo and deer wander freely. It has the ruins of a fortress and a half-timbered Normandy manor house of the 16th century as

Hotel Grand Cerf, Lyons la Forêt

Hotel de la Licorne, Lyons la Forêt

well as a most interesting Normandy Car Museum with all its exhibits of cars and bicycles which date from 1876, in working order.

The Collège de Normandie, situated 2 kilometres to the south of Clères, is an exclusive establishment run on the lines of an English public school.

CHAPTER V

Honfleur and Calvados

St Valéry-en-Caux, on the coast some twenty miles to the west of
Dieppe is a delightful mixture of resort, fishing harbour and market
town, large enough to have variety, but small enough to keep its
character. The centre was destroyed in June 1940 during the rearguard
action of British units as they were fighting their way back to the sea
after the collapse of the Somme front. On either side of the town,
monuments have been erected to the 51st Highland Division and the
French 2nd Cavalry Division.

In the Market Place a remarkable and very beautiful modern church
was designed by the architect Lopez with windows by André Pierre
Louis. Internally it is a lofty wooden and glass structure with buttresses

Church interior, Saint-Valéry-en-Caux

and beamed roof, the golden brown of beach leaves. The walls of huge panels of glass rise up higher as they sweep towards the altar and the eastern wall which is entirely of glass. The stained glass, yellows, blues from misty grey to indigo, and greens makes this a church of the sea, inspired by the silvery light from the wide skies of this coast. It is a combination of abstract and conventionalised forms; the glass is more brilliant and lets in more light as it reaches the altar where it portrays a graceful figure of Our Lady, with a setting of stars and angels' wings in yellow, the figures wearing robes of deeper dusty blue and violet. This occupies most of the space behind a very simple altar backed by a stone screen along which are ranged models of sailing ships. Climb up to the gallery and notice how the tones of the glass change and seem to trap a moving living sea and sky within the walls of the church.

The Gothic wooden Madonna was presumably salvaged from the old church.

Turning southwards to Cany-Barville a tract of wooded country follows the valley of the Durdent to Cany-Barville. Here the 16th century church has a 13th century belfry and 16th century carved panels at the entrance. In Barville, further south, the small church is particularly charmingly situated between the two arms of the river.

The road is most attractive between Cany-Barville and Grainville la Teinturière and passes through a beech avenue close by a Louis XIII château set amidst orchards.

By continuing on to the south-west, the route runs by minor meandering roads to Ouville and Fauville, then, crossing the main road from Havre to Rouen and continuing to the little village of Trouville, it branches east to Caudebec where the ferry crosses the Seine, and west towards Lillebonne and the new Tancarville bridge. An alternate way is of course to carry straight on to Le Havre.

But we have wandered away from the coast. We can reach it again at Fécamp, now an important fishing port for cod and far removed from its glory as a religious centre of Medieval Normandy. It has no longer much in common with the town where Guy de Maupassant lived for some years and used as a setting for some of his books.

Since Richard II's father had extracted a promise from him to build a Benedictine Abbey, he decided to erect one in Fécamp in the Burgundian style and he persuaded the Abbot of St Bénigne at Dijon to reside here with his monastic personnel.

The new monastery was the leading pilgrimage church in Normandy until Mont St Michel took over this role. It was so rich that it was called 'The Heavenly Gate', gleaming with gold and silver and shining

Pont de Tancarville
49

ornaments. It was here that in 1510, the monk Vincelli discovered the liqueur Benedictine by distilling herbs that grew along the cliff and he used its restorative properties to heal the sick. The famous liqueur is now produced in a vast building erected in 1892 as a kind of factory and much admired as architecture at that time The museum contains charters, books and the Roodscreen and statues from the original abbey as well as a good collection of enamels, ivories and wrought iron.

The Church of the Holy Trinity was erected by Richard I to house the relic of the Precious Blood collected by Joseph of Arimathaea and which legend tells us was washed up in a casket in the trunk of a fig tree. It is one of the largest Gothic churches in the whole of France and the interior gives an impression of immense space with its splendidly proportioned nave of ten bays and the lofty lantern tower which is largely responsible for illuminating the church.

The original church was rebuilt in the 12th and 13th centuries, after being struck by lightning, and then reconstructed several times up to the 18th century, restored in the 19th century and finally restored after the Second World War.

In a creek five miles south-west along the coast road from Fécamp lies the delightful little fishing harbour of Yport nestled at the foot of white cliffs with green meadows and cornfields behind. From the pebbly beach at low tide it is possible to reach a kind of miniature Norwegian fiord and swim among the rocks. The small Sirens Hotel has a lovely view of the cliffs and the bay of Fécamp and of the fishing fleet putting out to sea.

Etretat, 9 kilometres further west is still a fascinating place despite its great popularity. It was even more popular before the war as a great many British used to go there to play golf on the splendid course above the cliffs.

The cliffs have been eroded into the most fantastic shapes and have been described by over enthusiastic admirers as natural Gothic architecture. Even so, the curious arches and needles add a strange attraction to the pebble beach, especially in strong sunlight when they cast exotic shadows, and the caves and grottoes and pools are a never ending source of mystery and delight to children. The fishermen's quarter has some rather self-conscious traditional fishermen's thatched huts and the covered market which has been reconstructed adds a traditional touch to the town square. The church of Notre Dame has a Romanesque portal, with unhappily added tympanum, but part of the nave, built in the 11th century has Romanesque geometric and godroon decoration on the capitals of the columns.

Cliffs of Etretat

The curious cliffs of Etretat

I do not know of anyone who has seen the ghost of the three sisters who are still supposed to haunt the cliff near the platform in the cliff called the *Chambre des Demoiselles*. Legend says that the wicked Knight of Filleville was unsuccessful in his attempts to win their favours and so put them into a barrel full of spikes and rolled it over the cliffs. The three beautiful girls haunted their murderer wherever he went until, overcome with their dismal wailing and sad singing, he died and some say that now the white robed sisters appear no more.

Etretat is only 28 kilometres from Le Havre, a great port which can hardly be termed the countryside of Normandy, and yet is an essential part of Norman life and background as so many 19th century painters realised. It also has a splendid art gallery which does reflect the coast and countryside.

Duke Rollo was wise when he decided to settle with his followers around the estuary of the Seine. Under the Romans, Lillebonne, twenty miles from Le Havre, was a prosperous port, succeeded as a trading centre in the Middle Ages by Harfleur which was besieged by Henry V, in 1415. Shortly after the discovery of America, Francis I ordered the construction of Le Havre to replace Harfleur, and it was from Le Havre that so many Normans sailed to settle in Canada or Louisiana. In 1944 the whole of the centre of Le Havre was flattened by bombardments and shelling and more than 5000 of the inhabitants were killed. Undeterred, the Harvrais undertook the reconstruction of the whole of the centre of the city. They laid out broad avenues and built the new structures in concrete including the church of St Joseph which has a belfry 348 ft. high and a lantern with sides of coloured glass. The town hall square, designed by the architect, Auguste Perret, is one of the largest in Europe. Despite this ambitious reconstruction Le Havre has lost a great deal of the animation that it had before the war, but in compensation the traffic of the port is eight times its pre-war figure. To the south-west of the town are long lines of wharves for tankers and, behind them, oil refineries. In the past the largest French liners were constructed at Le Havre by the Augustin Normand, a Honfleur family that had been building ships since 1724.

By a stroke of genius the rivercraft barges can reach the port by a canal 18 miles long, constructed so that they can avoid the rough waters of the estuary.

In a sense Rouen is Le Havre's greatest rival, for the channels of the estuary have been deepened as well as those of the Seine so that ocean-going ships of important tonnage can sail up the river to the harbour installations of the Norman capital.

Immediately to the east of Le Havre, lies the suburb of Ste Adresse, sometimes called the Nice Havrais, with its beaches, its hotels and its villas. In the 19th century Ste Adresse was a health resort patronised by foreigners, including an exiled Queen of Spain, attracted by the mild climate and the glorious light of the estuary. In the second half of the 19th century it was this light which brought painters such as Eugène Boudin, with his wonderful feeling for light and air, a brisk sea breeze catching the sails and modelling the water into lace and grey-blue silk. This coastline also inspired his restrained ink and wash sketches of sailing ships—and his portrayal in oils of fashionable women with their flowing skirts echoing the swerve of the waves.

Later it was he who inspired Monet, the fifteen-year old boy brought up at Le Havre and encouraged him to take up landscape painting. Boudin also encouraged other painters from Paris to come to this region.

Even earlier in the century, the painters of the School of Barbizon, Millet, Théodore Rousseau and Diaz were influenced by the luminous skies and the light which flooded the countryside to such an extent that their rather sombre, heavy works were cleared of their gloom and began to take on more brilliant hues. But it was the Impressionists who were the best able to portray to the full the shimmering light, the flickering shadows, sunlight itself, and most of them spent a great deal of their time in Normandy.

The 20th century brought such painters as Marquet, Dufy, Othon Fries and of course the fashionable Van Dongen with his elegant beach paintings of Deauville.

It was largely to honour these painters that the splendid Musée des Beaux Arts was created when Havre was reconstructed.

Traditionally the people of Havre are energetic, gay and speak French with a lively twang. The cosmopolitans who direct the trade and commerce of the port tend to buy their clothes in Savile Row and sail their yachts over the channel to take part in Cowes Regatta, yet there is a tradition of the patronage of the Fine Arts and of interest in good literature.

The Tancarville bridge which sweeps over the Seine in a graceful curve to carry traffic to western Normandy is one of the most satisfying achievements of engineering in this century. A miracle of lightness and grace has been created out of concrete and steel. It is almost impossible to believe that it consists of 58,155 tons of concrete and 15,000 tons of steel and that by soaring 60 metres above the river it allows heavy tonnage ships to pass up to Rouen.

The idea of a bridge to span the Seine here was conceived as long ago as 1848 but for various reasons of economy, finance or impracticability every project was shelved. In 1926 a wooden model was made and was exhibited to try to encourage people to sign a petition for its construction. Following many difficulties after the War the bridge was finally completed and opened in 1959. It is now served by 33 kilometres of highways and has become indispensable to the communications between Upper and Lower Normandy.

Until 1959 Tancarville, which comprised an upper and a lower village, had only 575 inhabitants and very few visitors came to disturb its peace or even to explore the 10th century Eagle tower, the remains of the feudal castle. This belonged to the Tancarville family until 1320 and subsequently passed through the hands of several noble families. The modern castle was built in the 18th century for the Auvergnes. From its terrace there is an excellent view of the final section of the Seine valley as it flows towards the sea.

Although the bridge itself is so beautiful, it naturally gives rise to an enormous amount of traffic in the vicinity, so most people touring

Normandy and having seen it once, would prefer to take one of the several ferries across the Seine such as at Caudebec which will be described later.

On the other side of the Seine the route lies through the Forest of Brotonne to Pont Audemer, an attractive town of 10,000 inhabitants dominated by a wooded hill. This is a very pleasant place to stay in with its delightful, not too expensive, 17th century inn, le Vieux Puits, furnished with antiques, and a friendly Relais Routiers Cafe, just down the road for light relief.

Despite a good deal of damage in 1944, there are many old houses to be seen and there are attractive walks overlooking the branches of the Risle which flow through the town. The Church of St Ouen is worth visiting for its 16th century stained glass and the chance to compare this with the slightly garish stained glass in the chancel by Max Ingrand. There are some particularly attractive old houses close to the church. It is Pont Audemer that claims to have invented the sausage.

By following the valley of the Risle on the western side, the route passes through Conteville which, incidentally, gives good views of the Tancarville bridge and leads directly to the picturesque fishing harbour of Honfleur. But there is much to be enjoyed inland from Pont-Audemer and, along the east bank of the Risle lies Corneville where the Carillon at the Hotel des Cloches will be played on payment of a fee. This popular carillon started as a result of the great success of the 19th century operetta *Les Cloches de Corneville*.

Le Bec Hellouin lies a little inland from the river a few miles north of Brionne in a lovely wooded valley, watered by the rapid stream of the Bec. The pale yellow grey tower of the Abbey of Bec rises amongst splendid trees and the approach through the grounds is by the old abbey gateway flanked by two high roofed towers.

In 1034, an anchorite knight, Herluin, relinquished his splendid charger for a humble donkey and vowed to devote his life to God. In less than 10 years he had gathered 32 monks around him in the community of Bec. He was joined for a few years by Lanfranc the Illustrious who had abandoned his teaching at Avranches to live in the obscurity of the Bec community. Duke William met Lanfranc during his siege of Brionne in 1047 and later made him his most trusted counsellor and in 1063 he became Abbot of the new Abbey at Caen. In 1070 he was made Archbishop of Canterbury, the first of three arch-bishops from this community: in 1093, Anselm the friend of the poor, and in 1139 Theobold, the early patron of Thomas à Becket.

Abbey at Le Bec Hellouin

When Herluin died in 1078 he left over 1000 monks whose influence spread all over the country since the abbey had become a famous and much respected centre of education.

The abbey emerged from the difficulties of the Hundred Years War battered, but able to survive for some time under the patronage of wealthy families, the abbots doing little but drawing their salaries; even a royal prince—the Comte de Clermont—being Abbot for a time, decking himself out in 'habits brodés et galonnés'.

In 1626 some monks were sent over from Jumièges and brought about a Renaissance of learning, but finally in the 18th century the Abbey declined as a religious seat. The last Abbot of Bec was Talleyrand. In 1790 the monasteries were dissolved by the government and only a few monks remained; two years later it was taken over as stabling.

It was not however until 1809 that the abbey church was pulled down and sold as scrap, so that now only the foundations of the columns remain, but the cloister and the splendid tower stand to remind us of its past glory. The setting is one of green lawns, trim gardens, a lichened fish pond, which is presumably as old as the Abbey tower, and a number of white robed monks making a brilliant contrast amongst the green as they move about from the new Abbey established in the old refectory, itself a beautifully proportioned hall which contains some 14th and 15th century statues.

There is a museum of cars close to the entrance gateway. The town itself is most attractive and from here the road runs on to St Martin du Parc and is crossed by the highway to Brionne.

I must admit that we are taking a very circuitous route to Honfleur, but distances are short in Normandy and it is often an advantage to cover an area of attractive countryside if possible when travelling from one stopping point to another. It makes a wonderful short day's run to describe a circle southwards from Pont-Audemer, then go westward to get lost in a region of totally unspoilt deep countryside which stretches nearly to the outskirts of Liseaux. We then work our way northwards towards Pont l'Eveque and finally through the Forest of St Gatien to approach Honfleur from the south-west. In this area we are always prepared to lose our way. There is a maze of small roads, many un-signposted and all seeming to lead to anything but the place one is searching for.

A few miles beyond Brionne we turned right along the main Lisieux road, not a very exciting run until we reached l'Hôtellerie where we turned right and picked our way through narrow roads and glorious, lush countryside, pinpointing Ouilly du Horley on the map. At the Château we turned off to the left to Firfol with its beautiful old half-timbered manor houses and farms, its great barns and pigeon-houses built in orchards or fields of deep green and marguerites where the inevitable stumbling old donkey picked his way among the trees. But this is only one of so many villages and hamlets which have kept their deeply rural aspect, and driving or walking along any of the roads leading northwards will reveal some lovely old farm or manor house, ancient church or just simply a delightful stretch of peaceful countryside.

On this occasion we turned back to Ouilly from Firfol, then on to Moyaux, turning left through le Pin (which should not be confused with le Pin de Arras) and then on to Blangey-le-Château. Here there is a good church in the square with vestiges of Norman and unfortunately some modern excrescences. We then abandoned the deep country and turned left into the Lisieux l'Evêque road and drove straight on north to Honfleur, through the gloriously shady and rather mysterious Fôrest de St Gatien.

Since Lisieux has become the most important industrial and commercial town in the Auge region and the old town was almost totally destroyed in 1944, it can only be briefly mentioned in this book. Happily the 11th—12th century cathedral of St Pierre withstood bombardment and the beautiful details of its façade and the most elegant interior with a lovely sweep up to the lantern can still be seen intact. There arc a few restored ancient houses and the fine coffered ceiling of the 'Golden Room' in the 17th century law courts has been preserved.

In spite of the fact that Pont l'Evêque, halfway north to Honfleur, is best known for its cheeses famous since the 13th century, it has a fine flamboyant church of St Michael with a number of attractive old houses nearby and a 16th century convent of the Dominicans. There is a delightful old 16th century coaching inn, L'Aigle d'Or with its original courtyard of 1520.

It is only a short run from Pont l'Evêque to Honfleur, but much of the way is built up and the landscape is not exciting apart from the beautiful Forêt de St Gatien.

In the 19th century Honfleur prospered partly because of its flourishing trade and also because it enjoys a particularly mild climate and the surrounding region is exceptionally fertile. For the last 150 years the intellectual life of this small provincial town has been outstanding, for there were poets, historians, philosophers, novelists and of course painters, though few, if any, of the writers have achieved fame beyond the boundaries of France. Thanks to the shipping trade with northern countries, some Norwegian and English families settled in Honfleur and contributed to the prosperity and intellectual life of the town. In the first half of the 18th century many of the citizens of Honfleur emigrated to Canada and took with them the agricultural methods of their native province.

The sailors of Honfleur prospered in the slave trade, but a few of them became privateers to take part in the plundering of English commerce.

Honfleur was a major port until the 18th century when it began to decline as Havre became much more important.

During the Middle Ages there was a moat around the town and a small harbour, but in the 17th century the fortifications were pulled down and the harbour and a section of the moat linked together to form the Vieux Basin that we now see. It was then that the picturesque many-storeyed houses were built along its edge. Each house was only allowed a frontage of 25ft and as they were built on a much lower level on the quay than on the street behind, they often combine two establishments, the lower one being entered from the quayside and the upper floors from the street behind. The limited space on this

The Vieux Basis at Honfleur

sought-after site led to very odd construction of dangerously narrow and steep stairways and the familiar overhanging upper floors to give more room wherever possible, and it is this curious planning which does so much to give the town its picturesque and colourful aspect.

There is nothing to be seen of the original fortifications now except what remains of the 16th century *Lieutenance* or house of the King's Lieutenant, Governor of Honfleur. The Caen Gate which was part of the town's ramparts is incorporated in the façade looking on to the square. The vast 17th century warehouses, built to store salt for the cod fishing industry and also as a centre for the Gabelle or salt tax, can be seen in the Rue de la Ville which was once the main street of the town. They are now used for occasional exhibitions.

St Stephens (St Etienne), the oldest church in the town, begun in the 14th century and enlarged under Henry V, was taken over during the Revolution, first for a powder magazine, then a theatre, then a Customs House. It has now been incorporated into the Ethnographical and Norman Folk Art Museum.

The Church of Ste Catherine, with a spire which gives so much character to the skyline of Honfleur is the largest in the town. It has the same basic Seafarer's atmosphere as the very modern one at St

The Lieutenance at Honfleur

Ste Catherines Belfry, Honfleur

61

Valéry-en-Caux, although it was built at the end of the 15th century by men from the local shipyards. It was constructed entirely of wood in the flamboyant Gothic style with a free standing tower which has a curious spreading, boxed-in base as though constructed with wooden cards. The interior in the shape of a ship's hull and a number of ex-votos, nautical in subject, emphasize its marine character. It is well worth studying the 16th century carvings which decorate the gallery, and many of the wooden statues.

A large number of old houses and entire streets still remain and it is a delight to wander, for example, along the Rue Haute, outside the fortifications where most of the houses belonged to rich ship-owners and also along the rue de la Prison next to the church where the houses have been restored to their 16th century character.

Above the town to the west, Notre Dame de Grâce—a graceful 17th century building—is a shrine for seamen and absolutely crammed with votive gifts.

Honfleur is now no longer such a big fishing port except for local needs, but nearly a hundred boats still use it, more particularly to collect shell fish, and many yachts tie up here. The decline set in when Trouville and Deauville developed as bathing establishments and gay, elegant resorts. Then came the painters and the old port became very much a *Secteur Sauvegardé* and has remained so, although I believe that there are proposals to build a wharf on the river which will take ships up to 60,000 tons.

There is no doubt that Honfleur is rapidly attracting more and more tourists, that it is in fact almost the St Tropez of the north, and this does add considerably to its gaiety and liveliness, but I am always grateful to have seen it immediately after the war, sad though it was in some ways, but set in a vast area of mother-of-pearl sand silting up the harbour, a wonderful colour to set off the dusky browns and soft russets of the buildings with their sombre slate roofs and the old inn, the Hotel du Cheval Blanc, serving wonderful sea food and providing large, rather shabby old-fashioned rooms—it still does, by the way, but no longer shabby. There were no tourists, scarcely any visitors, just the innately distinguished inhabitants, hospitable and kindly and always amusing.

Along the coast road westwards out of Honfleur, lies the St Simeon Farm where so many painters used to stay and where a number of men who were later to become Impressionists, met.

Since the early 19th century Honfleur has been a favourite resort of painters, attracting amateurs as well as professionals, though now the

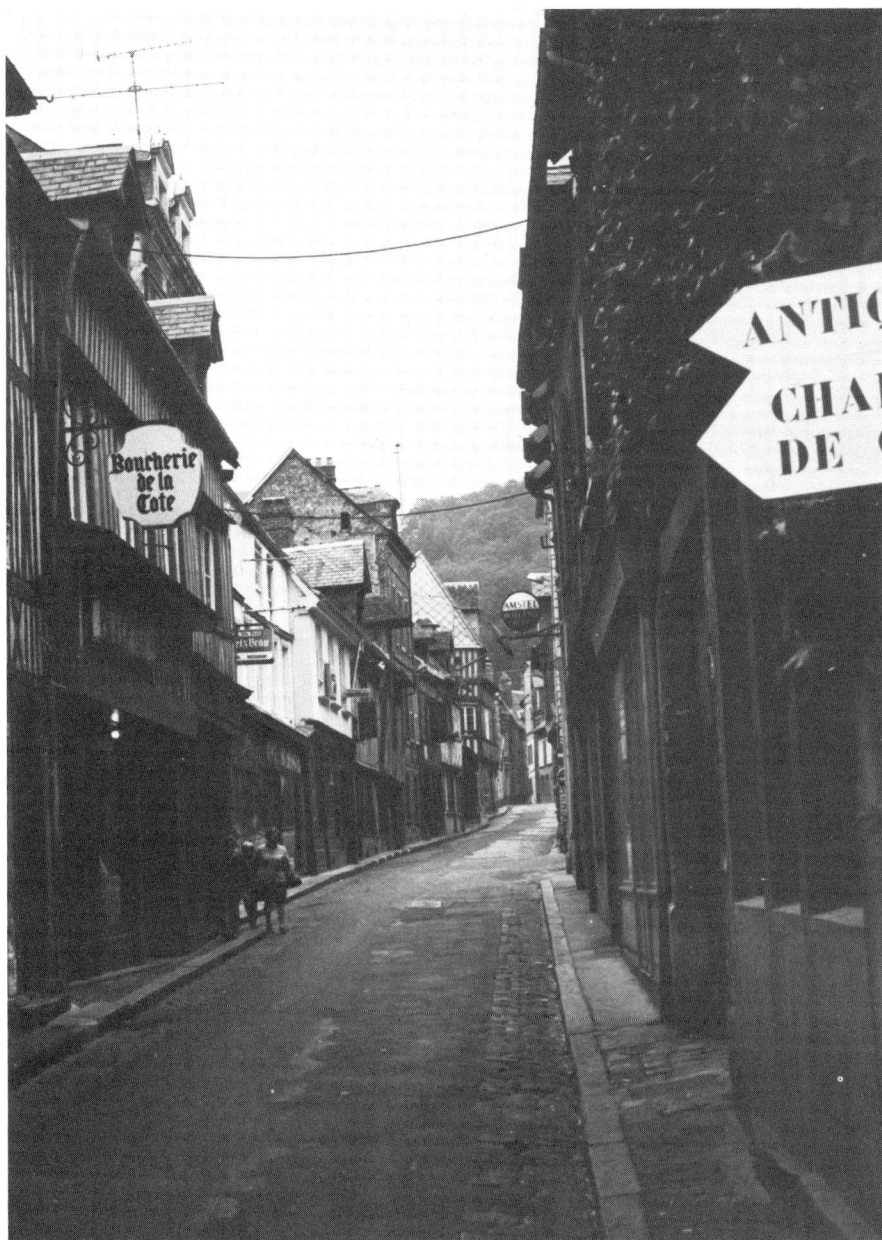

A street in Honfleur

An hotel at Honfleur

number of amateurs has swelled and the number of professionals has diminished.

Boudin, Monet and Bazille also painted the farm which included among its guests the English painter Bonnington, and it became the meeting place of the painters who were later to form the Impressionist Movement.

The coast road runs along the Côte de Grâce below the little sailor's chapel of Notre Dame de Grâce where a pilgrimage church has stood for centuries; a graceful building erected in the 17th century and filled with ex-votos giving thanks for miraculous escapes from the perils of the sea. It is still a place of pilgrimage and on Whitsunday morning the blessing of the sea takes place and on Monday a procession of small boats is followed by Mass in front of the chapel.

The road beyond runs through places with such familiar names as Trouville and Deauville which held such tremendous appeal for the fashionable of the 19th century and then became over popular. Once more they are gaining in popularity, largely as yachting centres.

Trees flank the road to Criqueboeuf and Villerville which climbs up onto the cliffs where there is a wonderful panorama of Trouville and Deauville, names which conjure up memories of the fashionable resorts of the 19th century.

As we drop down into Trouville from the corniche we can people the wonderful beach of fine white sand with Boudin's graceful windswept figures strolling along the beach with the fantastic, wide Normandy sky brilliant with the light that brought so many painters to this coast. It is still gay with holiday-makers who come as much for the yachting as the bathing and the casino, but has lost its pride of place to the even more fashionable Deauville with an equally good beach and an identical kind of wooden promenade, the Promenade des Planches, running its whole length. Deauville, of course has its casino, its race course and its yachts, and the town is planned as a luxury resort with broad tree-lined boulevards, flower beds and splendid hotels. Yachting, polo grounds, heated swimming pools, and even more amenities are under construction.

Blonville and Villers-sur-Mer seem tame after the luxury and splendour of Deauville, but they too have wonderful beaches. Then comes Houlgate and Dives-sur-Mer. It was in the harbour at the mouth of the river Dives that William the Conqueror assembled his men and his ships for the invasion of England in 1066. Though silted up, and

Yacht harbour at Trouville

full of copper alloy foundries, the town is still pleasant to stay in and has a really beautiful 16th century old inn, the Hostellerie de Guillaume le Conquérant. The 15th and 16th century market has a magnificent, well preserved timber roof and many other old houses still remain. The splendid Norman church was built mainly during the 14th and 15th centuries, but part of the transept is 11th century and the robust Norman arches contrast with the elegance of the 15th century nave. In 1862 the names of William the Conqueror's companions were inscribed on the west wall.

The countryside inland from Dives is very attractive with old cottages and barns, thatched and half-timbered houses in pastoral settings along the lovely rising valley of the Dives.

Cabourg, created as a fashionable resort during the late 19th century is planned with shady avenues radiating from the Casino. From the Boulevard des Anglais, a promenade running the length of the sandy beach gives superb views of the curve of the coastline to east and to the west along the landing beaches. It is indeed the last of the resorts to have been virtually untouched by the Second World War.

At Arbre Martin a few miles along the Cabourg-Caen road a turn to the right leads through Ranville over the Orne where the British 6th Airborne Division landed on both sides of the river and took the

Pegasus Bridge

Ranville-Benouville bridge (then called the Benouville bridge) across the river and the flanking canal. The section across the Canal has now been renamed the Pegasus Bridge in honour of the British troops.

The countryside is filled with sadness for the older generation since it so vividly evokes the horrors of British, Canadian and American sacrifices in killed and wounded, but for those with no heart-breaking memories of the Second World War, the somewhat unexciting countryside is pleasant enough though the coastline is now very much built up and has little of interest apart from bathing beaches. Some churches are well worth a visit and of course there is for many the over-riding interest of the war cemeteries, the war monuments and museums. Ouistreham, Riva Bella, Courseulles, Arromanches, for the British; Omaha, Coleville St Laurent, Grandchamp for the Americans, names which will never be forgotten by the relations of the men who fought there and liberated Europe.

In among these lies Port-en-Bessin, a lively and picturesque fishing port and seaside resort hidden in a hollow in the cliffs. It was here that in 1888 the artist Georges Seurat, painted his picture of The Outer Harbour at High Tide on a luminous, calm day with translucent water faintly reflecting the lovely shapes of the sails on the unruffled sea.

At Bernières stands a beautiful Gothic church with a spire much like those at Coutances and at St Etienne (St Stephen's) at Caen, and a few miles further west at Vers, a remarkably fine Romanesque tower has survived intact since the 11th century, though some restoration has been necessary. It comprises four successive receding storeys with bays and also retains the door above ground level reached by a ladder that could be drawn up after the inhabitants had sought refuge from attack in the upper storeys.

In the hinterland the most interesting monuments are those to be found at St Gabriel and of course in the still beautiful Fontaine-Henry which stands in the centre of a vast park planted with magnificent trees and built during the 15th and 16th centuries on the foundations of a 13th century fortress in an imaginative mixture of styles. This project has been entirely successful with its immensely high section of sloping roof, its huge chimney and turrets and spire of varying heights and sizes. The chapel is 13th century and so is the beautiful parish church.

The Priory of St Gabriel, to the west of Fontaine Henry and a little south of Creully, was founded in the 11th century and its existing 13th and 15th century buildings are now used as a school of agriculture. The courtyard is very fine with a monumental gateway and, as at Fontaine Henry, the roofline is fascinating with sloping roofs, turrets and gables.

67

The American cemetery at *Omaha* Beach

The Harbour at Port-en-Bessin

Another splendid 17th century monumental gateway can be seen at the castle of Brécy a few miles to the south.

A little south of Fontaine Henry the Romanesque church of Thaon has an unusual square bell tower with arcading rising out of a romantic wooded grove by a millstream.

Bayeux is a rather disappointing town, but then I first saw it in 1946 in a region of such desolation and sadness that even the cathedral, which admittedly has not the splendid proportions of so many Cathedrals in France, could not lift my spirits, nor even the fact that it was the first town in France to be liberated in 1944 and yet remain intact.

The city is steeped in history, for it was a Gaulish town, a Roman town and an episcopal city, and was later captured by the Bretons, the Saxons and the Normans. Rollo, the Viking, married the daughter of

69

the governor of the town, and William the Conqueror was in direct descent of their son William Longsword, but when Rouen became French, in the 15th century, the people of Bayeux remained Scandinavian and continued to speak Norse.

The epic of Harold and William the Conqueror is unfolded, albeit none too clearly, in the Bayeux Tapestry which is, of course not a woven tapestry at all, but embroidery upon linen.

The 'Tapestry' on show in the Baron Gérard museum, was almost certainly commissioned in England shortly after the Conquest by the Bishop of Bayeux from the School of Saxon Embroiderers and it is generally believed, though not confirmed, that it was intended to decorate the cathedral which had just been built in Bayeux. At a much later date it was named *La Tapisserie de la Reine* by the French and attributed to Queen Matilda. Every one is familiar with the design from colour photographs, souvenir tiles, table mats and even printed furnishing material, but this in no way detracts from the impact of the original in its lovely design, deep earth colours and dramatic force.

There is no such impact from the ensemble of the cathedral itself which has its 15th century spire spoilt by the 19th century addition of a 'bonnet'. The Romanesque towers had buttresses added to help support them which detracts from their original simple lines, and even the south transept, pure in style, is spoilt by the over-ornate gable.

The interior is exceptionally light and entirely harmonious; 12th and 13th century styles blending perfectly. The 12th century chapter-house has vaulting, reconstructed in the 14th century, with interesting carvings of grotesques. Near the church are a number of attractive mansions dating from the 15th to the 17th century and a charming 15th century turreted manor house.

CHAPTER VI

Caen and the Valley of the Orne

Caen is too large a city to be more than briefly mentioned here. As the capital of Lower Normandy it first appears on the historical scene when it served as the capital of William I before the conquest of England. William the Conqueror and his bride Matilda left as a memorial two churches, the church of St Etienne (St Stephen) attached to the Abbaye aux Hommes and dedicated to William the Conqueror, and the Church of the Holy Trinity attached to the Abbaye aux Dame where Queen Matilda is buried.

By a miracle the churches of Caen remained intact throughout the terrible destruction of the Second World War, although a great deal of restoration had to be carried out. This restoration and the removal of ruined buildings which obstructed a proper view of them has resulted

Walls of the Castle at Caen

in some of them being seen to the best advantage for the first time for centuries.

The vast church of St Etienne (Abbaye aux Hommes) combines the Romanesque and Gothic styles. The façade with its twin buttresses pierced by plain Romanesque doors is relieved from austerity by its splendid towers which soar gracefully into the sky. It has an elegance somewhat lacking in the Holy Trinity church (Abbaye aux Dames) where one might expect to find a more feminine appeal. There were originally spires to counter the rather squat effect of the impressive square towers, but they were destroyed during the Hundred Years War and were replaced in the 18th century by a commonplace balustrade.

Both churches have superbly proportioned interiors with very beautiful details and carvings.

The 18th century Abbaye aux Hommes (the original building was destroyed) is now the principal Lycée of the city and is famed for the excellence of its teaching.

In the 15th century the University of Caen was founded by the Duke of Bedford, brother of Henry V and his Regent in France. The new buildings are a remarkable achievement of modern architecture both for immense size and restrained simplicity.

The church of St Pierre, the third in importance of Caen's monuments, was erected in the 14th century and is notable for its superb Gothic spire and fine Renaissance apse which suffered considerable damage in 1944 and have been restored. This spire was so much admired in the 19th century that it was copied in several places in England.

The old church of St Nicholas, built at the end of the 11th century by the monks from the Abbaye aux Hommes, is no longer in use but it has a remarkable Romanesque doorway and the exterior can be viewed from the neighbouring cemetery.

The castle-citadel built by William the Conqueror in the 11th century stands proudly alone in the heart of the city freed from the surrounding buildings.

Apart from two wooden houses in the Rue St Pierre, the only remaining old dwelling house worth looking at is the gracious (restored) mid-16th century Escoville mansion built by a wealthy merchant.

The river Orne connects Caen with the sea nine miles away and from earliest times was used to transport the fine building stone which is quarried nearby. Indeed it was used for the construction of many churches and castles in the south of England, including parts of the

The Abbaye aux Hommes, Caen

Church of St. Pierre, Caen

74

Gateway to the Castle at Caen

Tower of London and of Canterbury Cathedral.

In 1944, Caen was the main objective of Montgomery's army, but a month passed before the Germans were driven out and two thirds of the city was destroyed. Many buildings escaped and casualties were avoided because agents of the Resistance guided the British artillery and aeroplanes.

The whole of the centre of the city has been restored, and many broad new thoroughfares have been laid out and planted with trees. The new Caen is a thriving, busy city surrounded by vast industrial suburbs which have been developed since 1947.

The products of the factories are transported by the canal constructed in the 19th century because the Orne was not deep enough to allow the passage of ocean steamers and tankers. In the present day iron ore and coke are imported and there are exports of steel and food products.

In spite of these changes the hard core of the old town has continued to follow a tradition of academic learning and professional skill. As in the rest of Normandy, the inhabitants are not given to violence and few Normans participated in the excesses of the French Revolution.

After the capture of Caen on the 9th July 1944, the Anglo-American forces began the enveloping movement which is known in history as the Battle of the Falaise Pocket. By the 25th July the Americans had occupied the North-Western part of the Cotentin and three days later their armies had reached Avranches. Gradually the German forces were being hemmed in on three sides, starting from somewhere near Mortain to the west, whilst, to the north, the Allied forces advanced on Falaise. By the 17th August the pocket had shrunk to only a quarter of its original size and eventually only about a quarter of the Germans made their escape, leaving behind them immense quantities of arms and materials. Altogether the Germans had lost about 640,000 men killed, wounded or taken prisoner.

One aspect of this operation has remained hitherto unrecorded: the Allies deliberately bombed villages and towns within the pocket, but the French inhabitants were warned of these operations by pamphlets and broadcasts. So, for the space of about a fortnight or even more, villagers and townsfolk took refuge in the fields under the guidance of their mayors, hiding in ditches when danger threatened. But since this bombing of the cross roads began as from June 6th and was intensified later, the villagers were on the move for six weeks. During this time the butchers killed off cattle, and so these unfortunate wanderers were well supplied with meat and also had enough milk, butter and eggs, but they were without bread and suffered worst of all because they had no salt. Astonishingly many invalids who were carried from place to place on stretchers and on ordinary kitchen chairs survived this ordeal, including a woman of a hundred who was said to be all the better for her experience.

The road leading to Falaise itself becomes more attractive as it approaches the city. The town walls and the castle of mellow stone, further emphasised by the almost luminous golden stone used in rebuilding and restoring the badly damaged city, make a remarkable impact.

Falaise was the birthplace of William the Conqueror, the son of Robert, younger son of Richard II, who was so struck by the beauty of a peasant woman, Arlette, that he invited her to the castle. She entered proudly over the drawbridge on horseback and it was she who bore him William the Bastard, William the Conqueror. Robert did not, of course, marry her, but later she did quite well for herself by marrying Herlwin of Conteville and their son was the Bishop of Bayeux mentioned in connection with that city.

Falaise castle is magnificently situated on the cliffs above the town which lies in a kind of ravine. The massive rectangular keep with its Romanesque windows was built in the 12th century, and the Talbot

Arlette's well at Falaise

Castle of the Conqueror at Falaise

Tower, the impressive round tower with its 12 ft. thick walls, was built in the 15th century and linked to the keep by curtain walls. In the St Prix chapel are inscribed the names of 315 of William's companions at the Battle of Hastings.

In the Square below the castle stands an equestrian statue of the Conqueror close to the Hotel de Ville which is on the right. Ahead the church of the Trinity and to the left a fine house has been skillfully restored in stone. A little below, Arlette's Fountain can be seen, where she washed the clothes and was noticed by the duke.

Holy Trinity church (l'Eglise de la Trinité) is in the course of restoration but even though the lovely statues of golden stone are damaged the general effect is most striking. The interior, entered through a Renaissance porch, is also pale honey coloured with 15th century columns decorated with delightful figures in a narrow bracelet; the ceiling is a deeper honey colour with pale, pale ribs and bosses, the chancel is empty save for a single crucifix and a plain polished wooden altar with simple candlesticks of brass shining against a scarlet curtain. The restoration has been carried out with superb taste and, since very little glass was left, some modern stained glass in an abstract design of yellow and violet has been introduced more or less satisfactorily.

Church of The Trinity, Falaise

Westwards from Falaise lies Pont d'Ouilly on the Orne, and at La-Fôret-Auvrey bridge there are views over the Valley of the Orne which the road follows from one bank to the other to Clêcy and then continues to Thury Harcourt. This region is known as the Suisse Normande, quite why, it is difficult to understand, for it has very little in common with Switzerland. I have seen no pine trees or lakes, no chalets nor rushing streams and certainly no mountain peaks, but it is nevertheless an attractive region along a winding river course with steep banks and an occasional low hill from which there are extensive views across rolling wooded countryside. An ideal place for hikers and anglers but on rather too small a scale to offer very much to the motorist.

Clêcy is the hub of the region in that it is situated on a curve of the river and is within easy distance of the most attractive parts of the valley and also has two simple hotels. The Sugar loaf 'height' and the 'Eminence' are within a mile or so's walk and both have wide panoramas which do not constitute heavy climbing.

As a centre I prefer Thury-Harcourt, further north, with its vast market square and simple Inn with the choice of two more down by

The Museum of the U.S. 101st Airborne Division at Carentan

the river. From here there is a fascinating excursion, *le Circuit des Crêtes,* across rather desolate but strange country with the pale colours of an abandoned limestone quarry and the earthy red of the mining installations. A wonderful little 11th century church of deep cream stone, combined with a marvellous pink-brown flinty stone, has a far-reaching view from its churchyard.

Contrasting with this strange almost lunar landscape is the little town of Aunay-sur-Odon, north-west of Thury-Harcourt. It was almost totally smashed during World War II and was incredibly swiftly and beautifully reconstructed by August 1950. The first impression of this rebuilt town is of the marvellous harmony and subtlety, the texture and colour of the local stone used in the rebuilding. The browns, yellows and russets, the luminous pale gold, the blue-green slate roofs and the beautifully planned flower gardens, combined with the skillful planting of trees, make this a really remarkable and colourful achievement.

North-west of Aunay I looked at the modern church at Cahagnes and was astonished at the lightness of its lofty concrete tower albeit rather arid in its setting. The interior was a different matter, a miracle of light golden stone, a wooden ceiling the colour of dried beech leaves, stained glass, abstract in design and glowing with deep earth colours, madder indigo, ochre, dusky green. All was enhanced by a simple bronze hanging crucifix and great earthenware jars of corn sheaves and bronze leaves set by the altar.

Continuing north-west through Caumont along secondary roads lies Ballercy. The lovely château there is almost a miniature Versailles: a well-proportioned and harmonious building, grey and pink, albeit now reached by a long treeless avenue and circus of houses. The farmland sloping away behind in its variety of greens and browns makes a fitting setting.

The splendidly simple proportions of the restrained architecture continues the approach avenue formed by the village street which widens into a semi-circle of annexes before it reaches the castle. The formal gardens were designed by le Nôtre.

The interior of the château has been kept in good order and is worth seeing, but I have heard that some of the heirlooms have gone and it is now a show place.

There still remains a fine avenue through the park to the elegant church built in 1651 by Francois Mansart and itself surrounded by trees filled with the song of birds.

A narrow road through the rich deep forest leads to Cérisy-la-Fôret, and its splendid Abbey. The impact is of immensely powerful, absolutely plain, lofty pillars with slight decoration on the capitals, abstract motifs suggesting stylised heads, then here and there a surprising little natural figure or two masks jostling each other into position. Here again the setting is superb. In the Monk's parlour the dungeon has 15th and 16th century graffiti, the 13th century Gothic chapel has a piscina and the Presidial—still called the Judgement Room—is now a small museum of furniture and manuscripts.

St Lô lies some 20 kilometres to the south-west and has the sad title of 'The Capital of the Ruins'. In 1944 only the badly battered towers of Notre Dame and vestiges of a few old houses remained. So needless to say, St Lô is now a modern town, but not all was lost for the new buildings have been planned to reveal the rocky spur surrounded by ramparts and towers giving character to the general impression of the town. The façade of Notre Dame still stands with its strengthened towers.

The Civic centre with its modern Hôtel de Ville and oddly incongruous old prison porch has a lofty concrete tower. This may not be to everyone's taste architecturally, but I found it graceful and light in its openwork design, and gay since it was decked in a spiral from base to crown with every tone of red and pink geraniums.

The St Lô stud, with its 230 stallions can be visited between July and February. It is mainly comprised of thoroughbred English and Norman horses and Percherons.

Northwards from St Lô and westwards from Bayeux, the Cotentin peninsular thrusts northwards into the Channel. It is totally different from the rest of Normandy and both physically and topographically more in character with Brittany or Cornwall than with the pastoral and wooded countryside of Normandy. It is wilder, bleaker, starker, has fewer trees but more heathland. Cosy half-timbered and sometimes thatched cottages of the east and south give way to stone and flint in silver and grey and black. Heather flourishes on the windswept heights and great, sweeping sandy beaches are patterned with black rocks.

From Carentan at the western base of the peninsular there is a fast main road to Valognes, or devious minor roads along, or parallel to, the coast for anyone wishing to visit more landing beaches. Valognes, a Gallo-Roman city, almost totally destroyed in 1944, has kept a few splendid 18th century stone mansions and is also a flourishing centre for the production and marketing of butter.

In any case it is worth while veering across country westwards after Ste Mère Eglise, on the main road, to explore inland and find lost

The Church at Ste Mere Eglise, scene of bitter fighting in 1944

hamlets with ancient buildings. Colomby, a few miles south of Valognes possesses a lovely 13th century church. Once back in Valognes cut north-eastwards to St Vaast and the coast and follow it as closely as possible to Barfleur.

St Vaast la Houghe is a picturesque fishing port dominated by its old fortifications erected by Vauban in the 17th century. The little islet of Tatihou is accessible at low tide, and the tide goes very far out along this part of the coast, leaving a great stretch of muddy sand and rock. It was here that in 1346 the troops of Edward III, who were to win the Battle of Crécy, landed.

Soon after crossing the mouth of the River Saire the beautiful 16th century manor house of Crasvillary comes into sight and a few miles before Barfleur the 18th century granite church of Montfarville has a 13th century belfry.

The atmosphere here is of Cornwall or Southern Ireland with a profusion of flowering trees, figs and tamerisks which flourish in the mild climate.

CHAPTER VII

Barfleur to Bagnoles

Barfleur is not exactly a beautiful place, but it has great character. Once a famous fishing port and, during the Middle Ages, the chief sealink between England and Normandy, it is now a seaside resort with a harbour mainly filled with pleasure craft which make a fascinating picture as they tip at all angles at low tide, reflecting their many colours on the shining sand. The rather stubby square tower of the 17th century church gives variety to the skyline of roofs on a slight rise along the promenade. There is a tiny inn facing the sea which used to be patronised by painters, and probably still is for it has marvellous views of the harbour and the sea. The Hôtel du Phare, more ambitious and more expensive, has a large garden, but my choice nowadays is the

Harbour at Barfleur in the Cotentin

Hotel Moderne which provides excellent food, and is furnished with antiques including a simple and lovely pewter dresser and some good porcelain. By contrast, the collection of paintings is only of mild interest and some rather odd modern additions in the way of lighting add a bizarre touch.

It was the shallow waters and swift currents along this shore which made the famous White Ship founder in 1120, when carrying Henry I's son and heir, William Atheling, his daughter and 300 other Anglo-Normans.

For me, one of the great attractions of Barfleur is the run of about two miles out to Gatteville. It is a complede seafarer's village with a square of granite houses and an old church, rebuilt in the 18th century, but retaining its original 12th century belfry. A really ancient and most interesting Mariner's Chapel and a memorial in the centre of the group completes the effect.

Restorations carried out in 1956 in the chapel revealed human bones interred in walls and beneath the floor, but excavation in 1958 brought to light skeletons buried beneath the paving stones in stone 'boxes' according to the rites of the 5th and 6th centuries and so it was certain that the chapel had been built on an ancient necropolis.

With the passage of time, different layers of whitewash had been applied to the walls and, during the last century, even a layer of plaster. During the very delicate task of removing these layers, traces of paintings were found. Brown outlines of a Figure in Majesty were distinguished, also red ochre dogstooth ornamentation round the windows, and this established the fact that they were executed in the 11th century. The whole area of the walls was decorated some time later, possibly during the 16th century, to judge by the traces of red and blue which are still visible. By removing the blocked-up windows which filled in the apse, the remains of a 15th century altar were found, and also among the debris fragments of a bas relief which had formed part of an even earlier altar. It has now been established that this little chapel, Nôtre Dame de L'Espérance was founded in 1070 on top of a Merovingian necropolis. In 1783 it became known as Notre Dame de Bon Secours and three years later, when a fire had destroyed the wooden altar and the roof, a wall was built to separate it from the knave and later this section was used as a garage for a fire engine. It was damaged during the Second World War and repairs were made in 1956. Ten years later, the Town Council decided to restore the whole building to its original use as a church and this exceptionally successful restoration and excavation was begun in 1967. The beautiful little

Virgin above the door was saved by the local sailors during the Revolution and its salt water washed form gives the impression of a seafarer's church which is emphasised in the interior. Inside stands another statue, a painted wooden figure saved by the local population and hidden in the belfry. Fragments of 11th and 16th century paintings can be distinguished on the walls, as well as deep pitting of the surface to ensure that the layers of plaster would hold.

After the awe-inspiring antiquity of this chapel, the other church, though interesting, seems rather tame.

The road to the lighthouse passes a second tiny little harbour and runs across countryside which might be Breton for its windswept aspect, but even in autumn the verges are covered with great waves of flowers: toadflax, dusky red sorrel, golden daisies, white marguerites waving above dark seaweed covered rocks emphasised by the dashing, foaming white spray and a dazzling blue sea. The lighthouse itself is most impressive in its modernity, elegant and immensely high.

Small roads along the coast and close to it give splendid views, and the road inland to Tocqueville is worth taking for a glance at the Château where Alexis de Tocqueville lived, the illustrious historian of the first half of the 19th century who wrote *Democracy in the United States* and *the Ancien Régime and the Revolution*. He was in fact born at Verneuil and married to an Englishwoman.

For those with a passion for Romanesque architecture there is a Church at St Pierre Eglise with a 12th century Romanesque doorway, and Tourlaville, on the outskirts of Cherbourg, has a Renaissance Château with an exceptionally lovely park of tropical shrubs and flowers and picturesque stretches of water.

However the coastroad is much more dramatic scenically and also has some architecture worth noting. On the way from St Pierre Eglise to Cosqueville stand three menhirs and at Cosqueville itself, which has a charming little beach, the church is partly Romanesque. About two miles from Fermanville the Cap Lévy lighthouse gives a fantastic view of the seaboard right round to Cap de la Hague, but if you follow the corniche from Fermanville to Bretteville, you will get a wonderful panorama without climbing the 113 steps to the lantern tower.

Cherbourg itself has little place in this book save as an embarkation port for Normandy, a lively trans-atlantic passenger port and the fact that its capture in 1944 made it a base for landing equipment as soon as it was cleared of mines and wrecks, enabling the Allies to close the 'Mulberry', pre-fabricated Harbours at Arromanches. For most visitors a drive up the winding road to the Roule Fort will give a sufficient and

Alexis de Tocqueville

very striking view of the town, the vast harbour and the protective breakwaters.

The War and Liberation Museum is of interest as is the Fine Arts Museum where one can look at the Filippo Lippi panel and some drawings and paintings by Jean François Millet.

The Emmanuel-Liais Park, created in the late 19th century is of interest to naturalists for its profusion of tropical—Gulf Stream-plants.

Along the coast at Querqueville stands a rather hideous Parish church with an equally unattractive cemetery distinguished by a remarkable panoramic view of the Cherbourg roadstead. But this is not all. Close to the church stands the beautiful little chapel of St Germanus.

St Germain or Germanus the Scot, was born in 418 and he landed in Normandy in 448, having floated across the channel on a wheel. This chapel dedicated to him was built about the 10th century on what was probably a Merovingian sub-structure for there is a funeral slab discovered in 1920 which suggests this date.

The chapel is a very simple umber-coloured stone building on the trefoil plan and its interior white walls are decorated with a herring-bone motif. There is an old statue over the simple altar. The view from the most unattractive churchyard includes almost the whole northern Cotentin coast. How dramatic and lovely this coast is, with its beautiful sandy bays with great rollers rushing in onto almost mother-of-pearl beaches, or foaming through black rocks and then inland pink and purple heather and golden broom covers the undulating countryside. Then comes the granite coast, austere and grim in dull weather, but reminiscent of the Scottish lowlands with miles of heather. Here and there straggle a few hamlets of rather dour little cottages, sometimes relieved by one or two with scalloped thatched roofs and the simple decoration of an Oeil de Boeuf above the door. The Cap de la Hague is a shade too menacing in its grandeur for my taste unless the season is mild, for gales lash the coast and great tides sweep in at terrifying speed as the water churns and boils. When visibility is good, the Channel Islands and the steep cliffs of Alderney lunging north-west from the Cotentin can be seen from this extra little peninsula.

At inland Oréville-Hague at the beginning of this tongue of land, a road leads north to the coast and Gruchy, the desolate place where Jean François Millet was born. The house is now abandoned but marked by a plaque.

Millet studied peasant life in this region and drew the austere, simple, almost primitive, peasants close to the earth and hardened to the difficulties of survival in this windswept land. His rather stark, but powerful study of the squat church in the village of Gréville is in the Louvre.

Born in 1814 and trained under a local painter at Cherbourg and later in Paris under Delaroche, Millet spent the last 25 years of his life in Barbizon still drawing and painting peasant life and landscape, and he became famous for *the Angelus* and *the Sower,* both a curious combination of earthy peasant power and both tinged with sentimentality.

From Gruchy, or rather back on the 'main' road from Gréville, the route runs more or less along the coast past the minute Port Racine and then on to Audenville with its view of another small port, Goury, which lies below.

The Nez de Jobourg on the extreme south-western tip of granite cliffs is so impressive in its grandeur and the splendour of its views from the heights that even an icy wind in September did not daunt me from clambering over the rocks to take in the astonishing scene of brilliant light, vast horizons, racing clouds and deeply shimmering sea, its waters surging boisterously and then delicately designing lace-work up the peaks of the rocks and spraying the grasses already swept flat to the earth.

Sandy bays and hamlets can be found down the coast with an odd inland village and one or two manor houses, the only protecting harbour being the small one at Diélette a few miles from Flamanville on its promontory. The Château built in classical Louis XIV style is also of granite.

Further down the coast the rock headland of Carteret between its two sandy beaches makes it one of the most delightful resorts of the peninsula. Being on the Gulf Stream, the climate is exceptionally mild and palm trees and other more or less tropical plants and shrubs flourish in the open.

Barneville, round the corner from the cliffs, has long clean white sands which extend on down the coast for some 25 miles from one village to another. Without very much character as villages, they are ideal for bathing, for children, for camping and caravan holidays. Their popularity and mild climate has been responsible for ribbon development which somewhat detracts from the pleasure of driving or walking in the immediate hinterland.

Barneville itself has a beautiful little 11th century church with Romanesque arches and capitals decorated with animals and figures. The fortified tower was added in the 15th century.

Further inland are some enchanting places to explore. North-east of

Cartaret about halfway to Valognes, Bricquebec is in the heart of the peninsula, a delightful little town, delightful as far as I am concerned more for its charming ensemble than for any great interest in the castle or even the Trappist monastery a couple of miles away. There is rather a surfeit of Abbeys and castles in Normandy and with many I find that their chief attraction lies in the fact that they often add variety to what might be a rather ordinary landscape or even give drama to a skyline. In any case women are not allowed into the Trappist Monastery so I cannot describe it.

There is an extremely attractive place to stay, situated in the castle precincts—the Hostellerie du Vieux Château—which is not at all expensive and in a partly 11th century building.

Because of the eastwards lunge of the Cotentin coast, Lessay near a deep inlet, is almost due south about 20 miles away. Here again, to stay at the Hotel de l'Abbaye and enjoy wonderful, but inexpensive food, is to be living almost in the Abbey grounds. This Abbey is not certainly just a distinguished decors, but a very fine monument restored with superb taste and restraint, one that it is worth making a long detour or even a special journey to see its lovely deep golden stone and the marvellous proportions of its deceptively simple design.

The building was very badly damaged in 1944 and might have been just another romantic Romanesque ruin open to the sky. Instead it has been admirably restored with the original material. Founded in 1056 by the La Haie du Puits barons, the exterior is a miracle of perfectly

Remains of the British 'Mulberry' Harbour at Arromanches

related cubes and gables and cones with deep-set round-arched windows seeming to move into perfect relationship as one walks round the exterior.

The interior is massive yet light with a golden glow, and here again the relationship of pillars and buttresses, groined vaults and round arches, the loftiness of the walls relieved by the gallery that encircles them and passes through the thickness of the walls. The very simple decoration of the capitals are similar to those at Cérisy-la-Forêt and so are some of the grotesque heads. But there is a feeling of life and movement all the time as one walks round the vast empty church because the varying perspectives fall into line with each other and make new and satisfying designs.

The robust restrained Romanesque lines of Lessay are in complete contrast to the elegance of Coutances which lies twenty one kilometres to the south across moorland countryside which tends to be repetitive. Whereas Gothic enthusiasts might call Romanesque Lessay square and somewhat squat, everyone must acclaim Gothic Coutances as elegant and soaring up to the sky in pinnacles of incredible lightness, not marred by excessive ornament, and superbly poised in successive tiers happily linked by supporting flying buttresses. The cathedral was built in the 13th century over an earlier Romanesque building and has a splendid lantern tower. The fine lines of the exterior are reflected in the lofty interior, yet this is somewhat tame after the impact of the whole exterior. There are however some beautiful 13th century (restored) glass windows and one of the 14th century of the Last Judgement. In a chapel in the apse stands the very lovely 14th century statue of Our Lady of Coutances.

The little town which is raised up on a low hill reflects its cultural and distinguished character as the religious centre of the Cotentin; in this splendid cathedral, one of the loveliest in France, in the 15th and 16th century church of St Peters, in the terraced public garden which slopes down towards the Bulsard Valley, and even in the excellence of the shops and restaurants. The devastation of 1944 spared the cathedral, but the town was rebuilt by the architect Arretche, who made such a tremendous success of the rebuilding of St Malo in Brittany. A visit to the public gardens, where there are some interesting flower beds is very rewarding.

The Abbaye of Hambye lies a short way to the south-east and is a shapely ruin romantically set on the edge of a park in the tranquil Sienne Valley. It mainly consists of an early 13th century Romanesque nave and a late 13th century Gothic choir with a lantern tower open

Cathedral at Coutances

Public gardens at Coutances

to the sky. The Convent buildings are in process of restoration but can be visited with a guide.

The variety of walks through the woods in this region are endless, but some sections are rather rough going.

Turning west again towards Granville and the coast, the route lies through Villedieu les Poëles, more interesting for its past history than for its present monuments, for it was here that the first commandery of the Knights of St John of Jerusalem was established in the 12th century. In the 17th century, it was famous for the skill of its copper-smiths who made frying pans and great round milk jugs. Now most of the craftwork is concerned with making copper souvenirs. However the bell foundry can still be visited where the highly specialised craft of bell making is carried on.

The 15th century church is a little too ornate for my taste—it is indeed 'Flamboyant'.

From Villedieu, a drive of about twenty miles west leads back to the coast at Granville.

Granville is a busy commercial port, but the upper town surrounded

The Harbour at Granville

by ramparts still keeps considerable character and there remain a number of old houses interspersed with later buildings in the lower town. Needless to say, there are splendid views from the ramparts.

St Pair, more or less a suburb of Granville, is rather less of a lively resort but has its own casino and good bathing; further south the villages of Quéron, Jullouville and Edenville lie along a magnificent stretch of sand with dunes backed by pinewoods. Glorious places in good weather benefitting from a good climate, but mournful in winter when they can be almost entirely deserted.

Carolles, perched up on a spur, is rather larger with its 19th century atmosphere, a promenade and villas with gardens backed by charming woodland walks.

Champeaux, St-Jean-le-Thomas and Genêts are sheltered, and the climate is exceptionally mild, but they can be very mournful out of the children's season (children revel in the shallow waters and miles of sand). These are splendid places for camping with children and they are all within easy reach of a number of attractive excursions inland as well as being near Avranches and Mont St Michel. The real advantage of the coast at St Michel is the tremendous recession of the tide which

The Walls at Granville

Mont St. Michel

exposes miles of mud. This can be very attractive in some effects of light especially when Mont St Michel seems suspended in a magical mist, but in grey weather and mists it can appear very desolate.

Avranches, on a promontary in a deep inlet, overlooks the bay of the Mount 15 miles away. The Botanical garden on the gentle slope of the spur has a viewing terrace with a fantastic view of the rock of St Michel with its shimmering reflection in the water or on the shiny surface of the mud and sand. It can be unbelievably lovely on a moonlight night—a dream castle suspended in an indigo sky.

The town hall houses a library of 8th to 15th century manuscripts and precious incunabula, mainly from Mont St Michel Abbey.

In the small square in the town, a paving stone is known as the Platform on which Henry II kneeled in public penance for the murder of Thomas à Becket.

A monument has been erected to General Patton who launched the great advance of the American Army through Southern Normandy; earth and trees brought from the United States have made the square on which it stands American territory.

Mont St Michel is in many ways similar to St Michael's Mount in Cornwall. It is an islet linked to the mainland by a causeway and situated in a broad bay. At low tide it stands in a vast desert of silver and gold sand and mud, and at high tide it seems to float on an aquamarine sea, mirror smooth for much of the year.

Mont St Michel is not only one of the most astonishing and beautiful monuments in northern Europe, but it holds the aura of many centuries of a romantic past. It seems probable that the island served as a refuge from pre-historic times, but it came into prominence at the beginning of the 8th century when St Michael appeared to the bishop of Avranches and urged him to found a monastery upon the island which was then known as Mont Tumba. To his surprise he found the site of the future abbey marked out by supernatural power and a miraculous spring gushed from the rock to supply water for the monks. The fame of the shrine was such that it was visited by thousands of pilgrims and was greatly enriched and enlarged by different dukes of Normandy, but especially by William the Conqueror after his invasion of England.

In 1203, Philip Augustus, who was at war with King John of England, ordered his troops to storm Mont St Michel, but they were only able to capture it when the buildings were set on fire. It is from that time that most of the buildings on the mount were erected. In 1427, it was besieged unsuccessfully by the English, and in 1469 Louis XI instituted the Order of St Michael which held its first chapter on the mount.

The area of the little city is small, but the central rock rises up to a height of about 350 feet above the sea.

Visitors are obliged to park their cars outside the main gates and then they pay a toll, from which the 300-odd inhabitants of the island are exempt.

The rue Principale climbs up the southern slope of the mount which is surrounded on all sides by massive ramparts. This little thoroughfare is usually crowded and lined on both sides by cafés, souvenir shops and three or four small hotels. This movement does not detract from the picturesqueness of the village, for after all, Mont St Michel has been a place of pilgrimage for well over 1100 years and the inhabitants have been catering for the visitors in this way for many centuries.

The most celebrated of the taverns, which is also an hotel, is the Mère Poulard, famous for the omelettes made from a recipe created a century ago and with eggs that are beaten up to a froth by three powerful young men in front of a large medieval fireplace. Almost opposite, the Hotel Du Guesclin, named after the gallant knight who was constable of the citadel during the Hundred Years War, specialises in all kinds of shell fish and other fish. I have often thought of staying here in one of the bedrooms facing the splendid bay especially as in the evening when the tourists have gone home, the little village regains its medieval atmosphere.

I find it hard to describe all the monuments that are crowded on the summit of the Mount. There is, first of all, the Abbey entered through the Guard Room, a large hall leading to the almshouse. Then a stairway ascends to the west platform from which there is a wide view over the sea. The church has a Romanesque nave and a Gothic chapel. Further on, the groups of buildings known as the Merveille, consists of the Guests' Hall, the 13th century refectory, the Knight's Hall and the cloisters.

It would be tedious perhaps to describe all the buildings on the Mount in detail, but certainly it is worth doing the round of the ramparts so as to appreciate all the splendid variety of light and colour which can be gained from different points on the height. At low tide the sand banks are laid bare quite frequently for as far as nine miles out to sea, especially at the neap tide when the rise of the water is as much as 45 feet. The incoming tide is so fast that it can be dangerous, and has caused many fatalities in the past, either by drowning or because the unwary have strayed onto the quicksands which are so deep that it is said that entire ships have been swallowed up by them. Before the causeway was built there were also fairly frequent fatalities among people who had not taken the precaution of finding out the hours of high tide, which, according to my husband's Norman nurse, could outstrip a galloping horse.

Further out to sea, the rocky islet of Tombelaine can be visited at low tide, but only with the assistance of a guide. It is noted for the rare flowers that grow in the sparse grass that covers it.

In the early Middle Ages, this islet was inhabited, for a family of the name of Tombelaine took part in the invasion of England in 1066 and they have left their name of Tombland in Norwich.

Mortain lies almost due east of Mont St Michel, but the main road goes first to the lively town of St Hilaire du Harcourt which has been totally rebuilt since 1944. It has a very gay and lively market, but the Gothic style church is extremely ugly although enlivened by frequent weddings carried out in the old country tradition with the bride and groom walking in procession round the town.

Mortain is totally modern and although much praised, to my mind it is none the better for it, though it is well maintained and in a most attractive setting on a hillside above the river Cance. A Grande Cascade of a waterfall plunges down some 80 ft in a sylvan setting. Nearby too is the old collegiate church of St Evroult's which was reconstructed of limestone in the 13th century. The rather heavy, gabled façade is lightened by three windows and the 13th century belfry is very attractive and simple. The Abbey Blanche, inhabited by nuns from the 12th to the 18th centuries, is now a seminary. It consists of a church and a partly Romanesque and partly Gothic cloister. The late 12th century chapel, the 13th century Chapterhouse and a storeroom are open to the public.

The surroundings of the town are particularly attractive with the forest of Mortain to the south-east stretching to within a few miles of Domfront.

This one-time border fort lies spread along a rocky crest and from the public gardens round the keep and the North Terrace on the ramparts there are panoramas of the Passais woodland countryside, and since many of the trees are pears, it must be a miracle of blossom in the Spring. It also overlooks the Valley of the Varenne, known as the Valley of the Rocks. In the past, the lovely little Romanesque church of Notre Dame sur l'Eau, on the banks of the river was the only parish church of Domfront although it was so far from the upper town. It was attended by all the Dukes of Normandy and Henry II had one of his daughters who was later to become the grandmother of Saint Louis baptised here in 1162. Still more or less intact after being disaffected during the Revolution, it was used for some time as a store and a factory. In 1836, the Ministry of Transport insisted on building a road from Mortain to Domfront through the nave in spite of the remonstrances of Prosper Merimée who was at that time Inspector of Historic monuments. Happily some reparation was made after the 1944 bombardments when it was carefully restored, but it still lies partly hidden below the new road.

The modern church in the upper town, St Julian's is, I think, quite the ugliest church I have ever seen. Built in the 20th century of concrete, it presents a hideous, tent-like exterior without any semblance of grace even in its tall dominating belfry. The interior is less positively ugly, but totally unoriginal.

However Domfront is situated in attractive countryside and by turning north just beyond Notre Dame sur L'Eau you will come to Lonlay l'Abbaye. The church, once part of the 11th century Abbey,

Church of Notre Dame sur L'Eau, Domfort

The Square, Domfort

with a 15th century portal opening onto the Romanesque transept is in a delightful country setting.

A more or less circular tour back to Domfront leads past a rocky height with a view of the Fosse Arthur where the river Sonce rushes between steep banks to broaden into a pool and then cascades downhill.

Bagnoles de l'Orne, with its lake and casino and the general trim appearance of a spa, lies amidst really magnificent and varied forest land, and has the fine Château de la Madeleine.

When Hughes de Tessé, who dearly loved his horse Rapide, found it was getting too old to be ridden much longer, he decided not to kill him, but to let him loose in the beautiful Forest of Andaine. To his amazement the horse returned to the stables a few weeks later, completely rejuvenated. He followed Rapide's hoof marks to find out where he had been and came to a spring where obviously the horse had bathed. Hughes de Tessé followed his example and was himself also rejuvenated. So we may hope, are all those who today drink the waters of Bagnoles de l'Orne.

From Bagnoles a most rewarding region of country is contained within a rough oblong stretching from La Ferté Macé eastwards to Sées, southwards to include Alençon, down to the border of Normandy and then westwards to include St Léonard des Bois and the glorious little church of St Céneri le Gérei.

This is once again a region where it pays to get lost. I always manoeuvre in roughly the right direction for my goal, keeping to the narrow roads where possible, and never failing to come across yet another dreamlike hamlet or little-known church or patch of forest or an enchanting pond or stream. Wending my way through the semi-circle of forests and woods just south of Bagnoles and then veering north, I make a long stop at Carrouges with its beautiful château to the south-west of the town. This is a wonderful château and holds its own with the best in France.

The 16th century entrance gateway or lodge is a superbly proportioned miniature château in itself. The narrow façade of pink and grey stone and brickwork has one window directly above the gate to meet the very deeply sloping roof pierced with another window richly decorated in the Renaissance style. The whole is flanked by round turrets with narrow windows in the same style, but the upper ones have only their pediments breaking into the spherical pewter-coloured roof. A single tall pink brick chimney relieves what might be too much symmetry.

Chateau at Couterne near Bagnoles

103

The Gatehouse, Carrouges Castle

This elegance of the lodge perfectly balances the rather later and more massive style of the Château surrounded by a moat protected by a very lovely stone balustrade. But even the castle has a kind of robust elegance if one can use a seeming contradiction in terms. It is perfectly proportioned with beautiful clear cut lines and octagonal and square corner towers in a glowing rose red shading down to buff at ground level, or rather at the level of the moat which is rather parsimoniously supplied with brackish brown water. Again, the severity of a deep sloping blue grey roof is relieved by dormer windows. All this is set against a park extending into the wooded countryside.

The gardens are tranquilly formal with a very green lawn bordered by neatly clipped, low box hedges. Avenues of chestnuts are approached by stone Renaissance gateways, pink patched green with lichen, with garlands and cornices and imaginative finials with wrought iron gates of a beautiful flowing floral design.

I prefer to admire the outside of this lovely place, and leave the interior unvisited, but it is unusual in that the lower storey is reserved for commoners and the very richly furnished and decorated upper storey is for the nobles.

Beyond the pleasant little town of Carrouges, the road passes through the Forêt d'Ecouves, one of the most lovely in Normandy; looking south-wards there are glorious prospects of rolling wooded countryside as the narrow roads lead northwards to join the secondary road to Sées. This again is a pleasant little town with one great monument, its cathedral, and a fine Archbishop's Palace.

I find Sées cathedral an aggravating structure, for I am continually changing my opinion of it. It is a splendid monument and a fine example of 13th and 14th century Norman Gothic; nevertheless from the 16th century and even in the 14th, it has been buttressed in a very positive way to prevent almost certain total collapse caused by mis-calculations of weight thrusts. This, naturally enough, rather clutters it up both externally and internally, yet the stonework of the choir is a masterpiece of intricate lacework for those who love the elaboration of Gothic, and certainly the 13th century stained glass windows are very lovely and so is the 14th century rose window. The graceful piers running up the columns to the rib vaulting, counteract what might be considered too much detail in the 'lacework'.

The church of Notre Dame de la Place has a good series of 16th century bas-reliefs and the old Bishop's Palace is a magnificent group

The Museum at Sées

of buildings with a courtyard opening through an imposing wrought iron gate.

Feeling adventurous, I decided to go north of the oblong to the Haras du Pin, famous for its stud farm, so I took the narrow road to Macé hoping to find my way to the Château d'Almenêches and the romantic Château d'O en route to the stables. A small north-westerly, seemingly un-numbered road leads towards Château d'O which is very easy to pass without realising it, as a large gate is the only gap in the thick trees and surrounding hedge. This is a fantasy castle of three main structures all built at different periods, linked by steep pointed slate roofs. It combines 15th century Flamboyant, early Renaissance and 18th century styles of architecture, but it is pale white and creamy and grey and reflected in the shallow lake edged with waving reeds and graceful bushes, it might be the home of the Sleeping Beauty.

There is certainly an easier way of getting to the Château by taking the main N158 from Sées, but then you have to be very careful how you turn off at Mortrée and the feeling of discovering hidden treasure is lost.

From Château d'O it is comparatively easy to find the way to Médavy and the D16, and then Almenêches with its Renaissance church, formerly part of a Benedictine Abbey. In this region the meadows and orchards abound with horses and from Almenêches a road runs north-east to Haras du Pin, or Pin au Haras, a stud farm founded in 1714, established in the stables of a mellow 18th century château and surrounded by meadows and woods it is famous for the horse show held here in August and on the second Sunday in October. Opposite this stud farm the Hotel du Tourne-Bride is a charming 17th century château noted for its superb and delightful interior, but prices, of course, are correspondingly high.

For more of this cheerful countryside with horses cantering about the fields, continue north-west to Bourg St Léonard and then southwards along the D16 through the Forêt de petite Gouffern with a menhir and then at Porte Mortrée we are back in our original oblong.

From Porte Mortrée the D222 passes three lovely ponds, on the right-hand side and just discernible through the trees; then the D26 through the Forêt d'Ecouves leads southwards to Alençon.

CHAPTER VIII

Alençon and the Perche Country

Alençon, with a population of 34,000 is definitely a town, but essentially a country market town and one of the most pleasing in the whole of France, so it does have a definite place in the Norman countryside. It is the principal market town of a large agricultural region watered by the Sarthe, and also engages in horse dealing with the Perche region, already mentioned, and to be described more fully later. It was a key town in the Mortain-Falaise pocket during the war. For centuries it has been famous for its lace-making and a factory was established in 1665 to set up in competition with the Venetians. The individual design of stitches underwent several modifications but it is generally characterised by geometric motifs, bouquets and individual flowers set against a diaphonous background. This lace was very fashionable in the 17th century and much sought after in the 18th, but it is now, alas, a dying art, and there is very little demand for it since quite good substitutes can be produced by machinery and man-made fibres.

Alençon is a welcoming town with a car park in the Place Foch, so enormous that it can surely seldom be full. This spacious square contains the 14th and 15th century Château which is now used as a prison, the Law Courts and the Town Hall. Work on this attractive, elegant building, designed with a graceful curve to the plans of Delarus, was begun in 1783; the little lantern tower was added in 1794.

The Town Hall houses a most interesting provincial museum and art gallery and it is well worth making a leisurely visit free from the crowds which often spoil better-known museums.

Short of space, like so many minor galleries, it has only been possible to display here some of the treasures which belong to the city. To mention only a few of the paintings: there are two by Philippe de Champagne, a beautiful flower study by Courbet, a lively little tavern scene from the School of Teniers the Younger, some Eugène Boudins, a still life by Fantin-Latour and a study of a dead youth by Géricault. There are two small still lifes which may well be by Chardin, and an

A street in Alençon

Hotel de Ville, Alençon

exquisite 15th century triptych of the Crucifixion in a magical, detailed landscape background.

The flower beds in the square are worthy of particular note: designs are presumably altered every season, but I was struck by the lovely beds of gold and silver and bronze flowers in front of the Town Hall and by the skilful design of subtly coloured plants in a large circle. Incidentally there is a Crédit Lyonnais close at hand which adds a practical advantage to stopping in this square, even if only passing through the town.

However, I always like to spend some time here as it is an excellent centre; there are a number of hotels to choose from and the Petit Vatel restaurant is outstandingly good, especially for its Moules Gratinées aux épinards, guinea fowl or turbot. It is not cheap—at the time of writing a basic 25—50NF or considerably more à la carte. To avoid disappointment, remember it is shut on a Thursday.

Even the ravages of war have not eliminated all the old houses and picturesque streets, nor destroyed the 14th century Flamboyant church of Nôtre Dame which was completed in the mid 15th century. The rather odd three-sided porch with gables, bell turrets and spires is, to

Chateau des Ducs, Alençon

110

my mind, rather jagged and prickly looking as though permanently under scaffolding, but the early 16th century glass windows in the nave are quite exceptional for the period. The church of St Léonard is mainly 16th century with an elegant nave and the beautiful restored 15th century oze house contains the local museum of Gallo-Roman antiquities and Cambodiam items.

The Préfecture is a fine 17th century building and, opposite, a double staircase leads to St Theresa chapel adjoining the house in which the saint was born in 1873. She entered the Carmelite Convent of Lisieux in 1888 and led the normal uneventful life of a nun. She died of tuberculosis in 1897 but she had already written recollections of her childhood which she began in 1895. With careful editing this book was published after her death, as the *Story of a Soul* and had a sensational success, being translated into many languages. Theresa was canonised in 1925.

There are still a number of half-timbered houses and delightful little lanes which make Alençon a fascinating town to wander in, with its antique shops, its pleasant restaurants, its riverside walk and here and there a lovely wrought iron balcony or an alcove with a sculptured Virgin and Child. Not only is it charming in itself but it is surrounded by enchanting Perche country: the Forêt d'Ecouves to the north, then the Forêt de Perseigne to the south-east and to the south-west, the little village of St Léonard-des-Bois and the nearby church of St Cenéri le Gérei.

I remember arriving at the village of St Léonard-des-Bois one early spring evening to be captivated by its rural charm as it lay in an enclosed bend of the Sarthe with steep heath-covered hills sweeping down to it. Wide fields alternated with woods and copses and, as I sat at the terrace of the local inn, I watched a man ploughing the deep red brown earth of a great sweeping slope, just finishing as the soft pink evening light faded from the sky.

A few miles away stands the dramatically sited Church of St Céneri on a steep wooded bank dominating the Sarthe. This is a country priory, not a great majestic Abbey but in spite of its small size it is planned on precise proportions and the interior is decorated with frescoes which are exceptionally fine for Normandy, though unfortunately they were over conscientiously restored in the 19th century. It is a lovely sight, whether viewed among the old houses of the village and the surrounding orchards or from below on the other bank of the Sarthe where it rises above the green waters on the terraced bank of wispy trees and makes a harmonious silhouette against the sky.

Going eastwards from Alençon lies forest land again; the forests of the Perseigne and of Bellême, the rolling, horse-breeding country of the Perche though there is nothing of outstanding architectural interest to be found along the main road. Bellême, the capital of the Perche, is pleasantly situated at the top of a small spur which overlooks the forest, but little remains of the 15th century ramparts though there are some fine 17th and 18th century houses and a Romanesque crypt. A number of good restaurants in the main street are reasonably priced, but parking can be difficult.

The forest mainly consists of really splendid oaks and beeches and makes excellent walking country; there is a large pond, l'Etang de la Herse, surrounded by trees close to the main road to Mortagne.

Tropical rain and hailstones the size of hazelnuts blinded my view of much of the country beyond this pond, but halfway to Mortagne lay salvation in the form of the Hôtel de la Cloix d'Or, provided with a broad-roofed car park in front of the entrance, facing you as the road swerved. Any refuge which did not involve walking a step under the hail would have been welcome, but this was quite outstanding as a restaurant and one of the best ways I know of passing a three-hour long storm. The luncheon was so good and so well-served—a marvellous country pâté, smoked ham, Truits aux armandes, fraises des bois, good barrel-wine and cheese and coffee—all for 22NF, that one might not have noticed an earthquake.

Continuing along the few miles of road to Mortagne, one comes to the famous and hospitable Hotel Grand Cerf, well worth a visit. A real hunting inn with rough wooden tables in the bar, two dogs and a cat, and a strange network of red-carpeted stairs leading to huge double bedrooms with plenty of chairs and tables and cupboards—and showers. The dining room is a delight of hunting tapestry covered walls with a pale wooden frieze carved with fruit and flowers and garlands. Delicate plasterwork surrounded the lamps hanging from the ceiling, stuffed pheasants were poised on the centre table next to a brilliant and sophisticated arrangement of country flowers. The food is delicious.

Mortagne is the former capital of the region and its brown-tiled houses are grouped together on a mound overlooking a wooded valley. Behind the Hôtel de Ville a public garden on a wide terrace laid out with formal arrangements of flower beds and further decorated by a huge bronze percheron representing agriculture, with Neptune and Ceres, gives a fantastic view across fields and hills and the Perseigne Forest.

The church of Notre Dame combines the styles of Flamboyant

112

The Perche country

113

Gothic and early Renaissance. This gives the exterior a rather lop-sided effect accentuated by the really ugly 19th century tower built in great quadrilateral lumps of heavy stone. The extremely delicate 18th century woodwork in the interior comes from the Valdieu Carthusian Monastery which used to stand in the Réno Forest, and the graceful little sandstone Madonna in the church porch by the tower is a reproduction or restoration of one from that monastery or is possibly a replica of a damaged statue.

Mortagne definitely has the atmosphere of a hunting town; busy and cheerful with vistas down every street out to the country through a medley of pink and grey roofs.

The remains of the Convent of St Claire comprise the Hospice with a 16th century cloister and an 18th century chapel.

Mortagne, like Mortain, Domfront and Verneuil was developed originally by the Dukes of Normandy as one of the line of fortress towns constructed to keep out the French.

Very little is left of the fortifications save the Porte St Denis which is now used as the Pecheron Museum.

The little river Avre runs through the Forêt du Perche and forms a number of small lakes linked by its waters. The white Château des Etangs stands on the edge of one of these which is surrounded by dark pine trees making an enchanting double image as it is reflected in the calm lake. To the east and near more small lakes, this time formed by the river Iton, stands the Grande Trappe Abbey founded in the 12th century in the forest. A Count of La Perche founded it in memory of his wife who was among those who were drowned in the White Ship. At a later time the Abbey was taken over by the Cistercians and it was here that in the 17th century the famous Trappist order was founded. Rebuilt and restored many times, it was pulled down in the Revolution but reconstructed at the end of the 19th century. The abbey is not open to women visitors.

A whole area of the Perche, roughly an oval from Mortagne in the north, eastwards to Longny au Perche and Moutiers, southwards to Nogent-le-Retrou then west to Bellême and north to Mortagne, is a region of lovely countryside where there are many attractive Manor houses and little castles which have been transformed into farmhouses. Even those not listed as architecturally worthwhile can look wonderful in a setting of rolling woodland and many can be seen standing a short way back from the road. The small castles are absolutely delightful, but they are really fortified manor houses built of beautiful coloured stone with turrets and watch towers. There are so many it is impossible to describe them all and they are best discovered casually, but one of the more obvious and typical is the white stone Courboyer Manor built in the late 15th century which stands on a hillside east of Bellême and a little north of Nocé. It has everything that goes to make a romantic small castle with its massive round tower, sloping gable roof and four graceful watch towers.

There are wonderful lost hamlets in the woods around Mauves-sur-Huisne halfway between Bellême and Mortagne and cottages near the banks of the Huisne and the Villette. We have meant so many times to rent a cottage or studio here, but have never had sufficient time to make it worth the effort.

From La Trappe along the valley of the Avre and through Beaulieu veering into the N12 is the obvious way to Verneuil but it is best to approach it north-eastwards from Mortagne or Bellême through the Forêt de Logny and the Forêt de la Ferté Vidame with their chain of wonderful ponds. This broad pond region which forms a rough triangle with its apex around la Ferté Vidame is full of fascination. Each pond or lake is individual, sometimes surrounded entirely by grass, pale or dark green, ochre or dusty red according to the season, or with dark pines or little wispy trees. Sometimes with lush grass and grazing cattle and, to complete the picture, a farm or barn with great sloping roof, or a miniature château with turrets and spires. At the town of la Ferté Vidame we usually take the very straight secondary road direct to Verneuil.

This stretch of road is absolutely straight, uneventful except for the farmsteads, the broad fields carpeted in spring with cowslips, in autumn a dusky golden ochre relieved by russet and golden trees, and later with silver grey bare boughs hung with mistletoe. It is, for us, the welcoming 'homestretch' when we have been driving far afield. We strain our eyes to catch the first pale blue misty outline of the magnificent tower of la Madeleine in the market square of Verneuil which is visible for miles.

Verneuil is in many ways the most delightful town in the whole of Normandy and this is to a large extent because the inhabitants have done everything in their power to preserve its beautiful streets and splendid old houses whether Medieval, 17th, 18th or even late 19th century, for the architecture of the Second Empire has a curious individual charm. The distinction of the people of Verneuil is also reflected in all sorts of unexpected ways. This town of 6,500 inhabitants, has two, really good bookshops, an excellent charcuterie, several cafés, and an amusing, lively restaurant in the square, where people of

The Madeleine, Verneuil

116

all ages spend the evening enjoying the relaxed atmosphere and friendly service. A few doors away the Ironmongers, run for centuries by the same Verneuil family, stocks an incredible variety of brass and iron door knobs, knockers, keys and keyholes and those decorative dull black hinges and finger plates difficult to get in England. Here, too, can be found a choice of *Toile cirée* – the old-fashioned oil cloth that used to cover kitchen tables, but which is now made of some sort of plastic lined with very thin felt—pink cabbage roses on dark brown, white marguerites on scarlet, wonderful for the kitchen or dining room. This kind of thing can of course be found in many little towns and markets all over France, but here in Verneuil it seems to have a special panache.

On market days or when there is a fair, when the enormous Place de la Madeleine is filled with stalls of gaily coloured goods or with booths and merry-go-rounds. Empty, it is a large, gracious square surrounded with half-timbered houses, small mansions, attractive shop fronts, and the typical and well proportioned county hotel, l'hôtel du Saumon, and the magnificent Tour de la Madeleine which is even more beautiful that its prototype, la Tour de Beurre in Rouen. It is rather less elaborate, the individual statues are finer and it seems to rise up in even more harmonious and natural stages to its final coronet. Floodlit at night, it makes a delicate, luminous silhouette rising out of the neighbouring rooftops. No ordinary rooftops these, for, quite apart from the buildings in the square itself, Verneuil has houses of such variety and such lovely proportions that their delicate colours of mellow stone and brick, their black and white panelling of timber, their decorative turrets ennoble the least of its streets.

Verneuil, as I mentioned earlier, was once a frontier town and the scene of some of the fiercest battles of the Hundred Years' War. The Medieval ramparts are now transformed into peaceful, shady walks. Indeed one can stroll along the banks of the Avre and its tributary the Iton, past the Tour Grise, an enormously powerful-looking keep built by Henry I of England in 1120, and then turn into the old streets which lead north to the place de la Madeleine and west to the church of Notre Dame which, unlike the Madeleine is commonplace outside, but inside is filled with masterpieces of sculpture including a most moving painted wooden statue of the Virgin carved in the 13th century, and a number of 15th and 16th century stone statues of saints.

The Ecole des Roches, about two miles to the west of Verneuil, was founded by Edmond de Moleyns on the model of an English public school, though on more humanitarian lines, in order to give its pupils a training in character and physical development as well as academic teaching. Its place in France corresponds approximately to Eton and Winchester together, and no boy is admitted unless the antecedents of his parents are really honourable, and Christian, catholic or protestant. The success of this venture is proved by the number of old boys whose names figure in the French Who's Who and, to a lesser degree, in the Almanach de Gotha. More recently the school has become co-educational, for there are one or two houses for girls only, who participate in most of the activities of the boys. Though most of the buildings are without architectural merit, they are scattered about in the woods and meadows over an area of about a thousand acres.

The N840 leads directly to Breteuil-sur-Iton, encircled by the river and on the edge of the Forest of the same name which stretches out to the west. The church has retained some early features including the transept pillars which date back to William the Conqueror.

The road continues almost directly north to Conches, the last few miles going through the Forêt de Conches which is continuous with the Forêt de Breteuil.

Situated on a spur encircled by the river Rouloir the town of Conches-en-Ouche is famous for its church of St Foy with its magnificent 15th and 16th century stained glass windows inspired by Dürer's engravings.

Early in the 11th century Roger I, Lord of Conches, at that time called Douville, went to fight the Moors in Spain and having heard of the relics of the child Saint Foy, made a pilgrimage to Conques-en-Rouergues where they were venerated, on his return journey to France.

Roger is said to have stolen the relics, taken them to his home town and to have built a church dedicated to the Saint. He then re-named the town Conches. The original church was replaced by the present elegant Gothic building in the 15th century. The tall spire had to be rebuilt in the middle of the 19th century and has, once again, just been restored.

The general effect of the stained glass is most impressive, more especially as there is comparatively little of a very high order in Normandy. Filling the windows on both sides of the church they lead up majestically to the choir with its lancet windows gleaming between slender columns which rise up to a beautiful vaulted ceiling. To the left of the choir is a very finely carved wooden doorway and to the right at the end of the south aisle, the Alabaster Triptych of the Passion was carved in minute detail with great sensitivity by English craftsmen of the 15th century.

The terracotta Stations of the Cross are attractively naïve and the modern tapestry of Christ in Majesty is the work of Marie Chantereine, a local artist.

From the terrace on the south side of the church there is a very fine view of the chancel roof and also, looking down from the parapet, a prospect of the peaceful valley. A gate through the town hall, leads to a delightful little garden where stands the ruined keep and several battered towers of the Castle built here in the 12th century by Roger III and shortly afterwards besieged and taken by Philip Augustus. It fell alternately into the hands of the French and the English during the Hundred Years' War, and it finally dropped into decay when the Huguenots of Evreux took it in 1590.

Evreux, 18 kilometres to the east, with a present population of over 45,000 is scarcely countryside. It was repeatedly battered during its long history, but has now become a prosperous agricultural market centre for the surrounding region, having repaired the ravages of the Second World War. It has been rebuilt as a modern city yet imaginative planning has preserved as many as possible of its old monuments and created a kind of reservation along the banks of the Iton where pedestrians can stroll away from the traffic. The river itself which was little more than a refuse dump in 1939 has been cleared and canalised between walls built of old stones. Gardens and a walk now lie at the foot of the old Gallo-Roman ramparts and it is possible to make a picturesque tour of the centre of the old city from the elegant 15th century clock tower to the Cathedral which is still under reconstruction, but is well worth visiting for its fine glass, wood carvings and wrought iron. The Bishopric alongside with its window pediments and staircase tower is now a museum.

The Church of St Taurinus, to the west of the cathedral, dating from the 14th and 15th century, contains a 13th century reliquary of gilt, silver and enamels. Donated by Saint Louis, it is one of the most beautiful examples of the French silversmith's art.

Since our route north from Conches tends to zigzag westwards and lies west of Rouen, the 18 kilometre run eastwards to Evreux is a definite diversion and, except for those particularly interested in reconstruction and restoration or in seeing the Saint Taurinus Shrine, it is more enjoyable to take a wandering westwards route from Conches using the local roads, some of which are very narrow although well surfaced, where the signposts have a habit of being broken or twisted as an added hazard.

The lovely Château of Beaumesnil can easily be reached by the main road to Bernay where it lies just outside the hamlet of the same name. It is a superb example of Louis XIII style of architecture, and stands picturesquely reflected in a moat with vast gardens stretching on either side. From here an inviting forest road leads eastwards to Beaumont-le-Roger, but those who have had a surfeit of châteaux may do well to forget Beaumesnil and make their way, as directly as the maze of enchanting small roads will let them, from Conches to Beaumont where the Church of St Nicholas is in course of restoration. Built during the 14th and 16th centuries, it was damaged during the war and is a splendid example of the successful supplementing of the fine old windows with modern ones. These are of sombre beauty in leaden blue, yellow, green and dusky rose spreading a soft radiance throughout the church. A number of early polychrome statues and some plain mellow stone ones are of especial interest, and add to the atmosphere of restrained colour and decoration in this church, beautifully situated above the waters of the Risle, an atmosphere further enhanced by the romantic ruins of a 13th century priory a mile or so away on a broad grassy slope framed by trees.

The easiest way to Champ de Bataille is through le Neubourg which itself is attractive with a lively market and a 16th century church, but it is far more enjoyable to thread a more westerly way by passing the little town and passing through very quiet, uneventful countryside save that here and there stand small country churches with the traditional yew trees planted in the graveyard to cleanse the atmosphere, and a number of ancient castles adding a picturesque touch.

I find the Château of Champ de Bataille more impressive than attractive at first sight. It is immense and set on a rather dull plain, though built in a deer park. Yet on closer inspection it is a magnificent architectural achievement having a Louis XIV aspect although built of brick. The enormous south portico with its broken pediment seems more like a triumphal arch standing out against the sky and, as one looks at the 250 ft long wings which face each other, one for commoners, the other for nobles, one is struck by the splendour of the planning, the sweeping horizontal lines adding to the impression of great size and spaciousness, giving somewhat the same effect afforded by the proportions of Versailles.

The parish church of Harcourt, nearby to the east, but again across tricky roads, has a beautiful 15th century apse, but it is the vast park to the north with its medieval castle entrance which is of greater interest. Enormous cedar trees begin the avenue which leads to the fortified entrance flanked by towers and surrounded by a broad moat.

Chateau of Champ de Bataille

121

From this region seek for a signpost to Bourgtheroulds or Elbeuf, at either of which the signposting is clear to Rouen or to the ferries across the Seine.

CHAPTER IX

The Valley of the Seine

Of all the riverside cities of Normandy, Caudebec is by far the most beautiful in spite of the fact that a large part of this little city was burnt down by German bombing in 1940. Carefully restored, it has of course lost many ancient streets and monuments but still retains a great deal of its former charm.

The city has always been prosperous because of the traffic on the Seine which in the Middle Ages, carried passengers and supplies of food as far as Paris.

There are two ideal ways of coming to Caudebec: the first is by the D33 from Fécamp which passes through the beautiful forest of Maulévrier and then suddenly there comes a steep descent with a prospect of red-tiled roofs below and the broad shining surface of the Seine. Alternatively, it is equally impressive to approach by ferry from the far side of the river because of the gay waterfront and the gardens that line it. In past years hundreds of visitors used to come to Caudebec at the time of the equinox to see the Bore or *mascaret* when the great tides are running and the huge wave rushes up the Seine. Theoretically this phenomenon can no longer be seen because of the new channels which have been cut in the estuary of the river but it is beginning to manifest itself once more, though not with equal regularity.

In the nearby village of Villequier, there is a museum to Victor Hugo's daughter who was drowned with her husband by the *mascaret*. On display are family letters between the poet and his daughter and a number of objects and traditional pieces of Norman furniture. The tombs of Charles Vacquerie and his wife Leopoldine, Victor Hugo's daughter, are in the church. The greatest charm of Villequier however is the riverside walk and the quay where the marine pilots take over ships from the upstream pilots.

However, this is one of many easy excursions from Caudebec which is quite attractive enough to be worth lingering in, and forms a good centre for visiting the numerous places of interest along and in the deep loops of the Seine.

But to begin with the town of Caudebec. The outstanding monument of the Church of Notre Dame was praised by Henry IV of France as the 'prettiest chapel in his kingdom', but he added that it was a jewel with a commonplace setting, so he obviously did not think much of the city itself, though, to judge by the few old houses left standing by the church, it must have had considerable charm and certainly the setting in a wider sense, the surrounding countryside of river and forest, is admirable.

Although the extensive fire of 1940 destroyed the medieval aspect of the city, the church, built in 1425 upon the foundations of an earlier edifice, escaped practically intact, even though the heat was so intense that the bells began to melt and started pealing of their own accord. It was constructed between 1425 and 1539, a period when the French kings had abandoned this part of the country to the English and had settled on the banks of the Loire. In 1440 the direction of the work was taken over by a prominent architect, Guillaume Letellier, who was responsible for the choir and the ambulatory with its side chapels including the famous pendentive keystone, supported only by the lateral arches and forming a drop of 13 feet. His remains were buried in the chapel beneath the keystone on his death in 1485. Le Tellier's work was taken on by a new architect, probably Thomas Theroulde. He was responsible for the beautiful spire erected between 1490 and 1520, the two last bays and the great portal which was completed in 1539. The west façade is pierced by a very beautiful rose window.

Twenty-three years later the Iconoclasts of Rouen defaced the statues of the portal and, in 1793, the citizens replaced the tympanum. In the 19th century, the spire was struck by lightning and had to be restored.

Within the church is a wealth of wood and stone carving and a number of panels with fine detail, but above all, the 16th century stained glass windows cannot fail to attract attention by their beauty, their diversity of origin and subject matter and by their glowing colour, although some sections are rather garish.

It has been established that some of the glass came from Flanders, some from itinerant guilds of craftsmen established by Charles VI, some from Caudebec itself and some also from England.

The stained glass depicting the Tree of Jesse in the baptistry chapel is very obviously of two different periods, the lower half probably made by Lafont from Flanders and the upper part depicting the Virgin, is a 19th century replacement commonplace in design and crude in colour. The stained glass above the north portal was made in England and donated by the last of the English captains commanding Caudebec during the Hundred Years' War. Is it possible that it came from Beckley near Rye in Sussex? Apparently there were a number of artists working in stained glass at that time and many inhabitants of the village bear the name of Glazier.

In the Chapel of the Holy Sepulchre a minutely carved recumbent figure of Christ lies beneath a fine 16th century baldachin. The large statues here all come from the nearby Abbey of Jumièges.

Two original 13th century gable walls of the Templar's House still stand but the interior has been considerably altered and houses a museum of local historical objects of rather moderate interest.

Two hotels on the water front serve excellent food, but the noise of the traffic in the front rooms is infernal, so, for anything but an overnight stop, a hotel away from the river is preferable, or, when in funds even the luxurious Manoir de Rétival, a beautiful Manorhouse, slightly inland, but set in a park which overlooks the Seine and the Forêt de Brotonne and is renowned for its food, its service and its elegant ambiance.

Caudebec provides endless opportunities for short or long excursions in the region, although there is a good deal of traffic in the immediate vicinity and heavy lorries take the ferry and rumble along the highways in all directions. Nevertheless, after a mile or so, they all disperse and the calm riverside, pastoral and wooded country lies waiting to be explored.

Yvetot lies about a third of the way between Caudebec and the coast at St Valéry-en-Caux or considerably further from Dieppe, but even then it is an easy short excursion or can be taken in on a morning's drive back to the Channel port.

Despite its very modern church, there is a romantic atmosphere about the town of Yvetot made famous as the legendary capital of a totally imaginary realm by the Song of the 19th century poet Béranger, Le Roi d'Yvetot, a satire against Napoleon.

Since Yvetot was three-quarters destroyed in the Second World War, and in earlier centuries its wooden thatched houses were always a prey to fire, there are few ancient remains to attract visitors, but like Dieppe it does possess a collection of ivories housed in the Hôtel de Ville and like St Valéry-en-Caux it has a magnificent modern church which was inaugurated in 1956 and marks one of the most important stages in the replanning of the town.

The Church of St Pierre was designed by Yves Marchand, a young architect from Paris who conceived it as a completely round church built in concrete and glass. It is a most astonishing and beautiful achievement. A light, but immensely strong, shallow dome covers the circular church, its walls being composed of slender concrete pillars supporting and dividing tall stained glass windows rising up from the plain concrete foundation to the rows of panels below the roof. A huge panel carved in high relief surmounts the entrance and reaches up to the dome. St Peter, as the central figure, is represented as a fisherman with a net over his shoulder against a pattern of network. This is flanked by smaller panels of bas-reliefs of episodes in the apostle's life. To the right of the entrance, an openwork square concrete campanile rising up to a height of over a hundred feet, is linked to the main church by a baptistry.

Yves Marchand must share the honours for the success of this building with Max Ingrand who was responsible for the windows which are the main feature of the interior and give it so much vitality and colour. A gleaming radiance, broken only by thin pillars of concrete, illuminates the church, pale and sombre in colour at the entrance and strengthening and brightening as it curves behind the altar into brilliant reds, purples, gold and blue to the section of the Crucifixion.

The High Altar is absolutely plain save for six simple bronze candlesticks and a tabernacle of modern design. Indeed, all the furnishings are kept to a minimum and the keynote is simplicity, for all the splendour and decoration is provided by the stained glass.

The vast round nave can hold eight hundred people but there is a smaller chapel divided by an ambulatory and a glass wall from the nave. This can take a congregation of two hundred and is large enough for general use. The statue of the Virgin, saved from the ruins of the previous church, is preserved here.

Incidentally on the other side of the crossroads an exceptionally good delicatessen produces an outstanding selection of pâtés, cooked meats and quiches.

Eastwards from Caudebec and on the same bank of the river are a number of sights well worth visiting both for their intrinsic interest and the beauty of the settings. Roughly speaking the main Rouen road winds within a few miles of three of the most attractive: St Wandrille, Jumièges and St Martin de Boscheville.

The first of these is along a turning to the left shortly after leaving Caudebec. The Abbey of St Wandrille is one of the most romantic and historic buildings in Normandy. Established in the Fontenelle Valley in 649, it became famous under that name, but later took the name of its

The Cloisters at Jumièges

founder, St Wandrille.

Count Wandrille, after celebrating his marriage at King Dagobert's court, decided to become a hermit, whilst his wife became a nun. After wandering to several monasteries, he returned to Rouen to be ordained and was much admired for his saintliness and also for his physical beauty; so much so, that he was called God's Athlete and Fontenelle became the 'Valley of the Saints' and the Abbey still has its celebration of All Saints of the Monastery.

The Epic of the Abbots of Fontenelle, written in 831, was the first history of a western Monastery. Since its foundation the abbey was constantly despoiled and reconstructed, but ruins of the splendid Gothic Abbey church still remain with the wonderful clustered columns supporting the springing of the transept roof now open to the sky. The 14th and 15th century cloisters are a most delightful feature, rare in Normandy; a niche contains a much revered 14th century statue of Our Lady of Fontenelle. Scenes of the new testament decorate the blind arcade of a decorative lavabo with six taps built into the wall to the right of the refectory. It is partly Gothic and partly Renaissance in style.

The buildings became a Benedictine Abbey in the 10th century when monks began to rebuild the ruins after the havoc left by the Vikings, partly, it is believed, with the stones of the ranges of seats in the Roman theatre at Lillebonne.

The Wars of Religion brought about only a temporary decline but the Revolution led to the dispersal of the monks and the Monastery fell into ruin. During the 19th century the Abbey had various owners including the Englishman with a foreign title, the Marquis of Stacpoole, who was responsible for building the monumental gateway, (the actual Abbey is entered through a 15th century door surmounted by a pelican) and the author, Maurice Maeterlinck, who lived there for some years.

In 1931, the abbey was given back to the Benedictines who now live in buildings which were added over the years.

The present monastery church, where Mass is celebrated with the Gregorian chant, is an old 15th century tithe barn which was brought piecemeal from its original setting in the Eure and re-erected here in 1969.

A path along the Abbey wall leads to the St Saturninius Chapel, a little oratory rebuilt in the 10th century, possibly over the ruins of a Merovingian chapel, and given a new façade in the 16th century.

After the turning to St Wandrille, the Rouen road runs more or less

Remains at Jumièges

parallel to the river and through the Forêt du Trait where the smaller road to Jumièges is clearly signposted.

Everyone is familiar with outlines of the Abbey of Jumièges from photographs and posters, but this in no way detracts from the fact that the beautiful lines of this magnificent and very beautiful ruin cannot fail to move even the least architecturally-minded visitor.

St Philibert founded the Abbey in the 7th century, establishing in the forest of that name a peaceful colony of monks who drained the marshy tracts, cleared away the rocks and transformed what had been a wilderness into a garden. His efforts to improve the conditions of the people brought him into displeasure with the Court and he was turned out of Jumièges, but he continued to found monasteries elsewhere and he had so firmly established the original monks that their number had grown to 900 by the end of the century.

Like St Wandrille, Jumièges was over-run by the Vikings, the inmates were scattered and only two monks were left. William Longsword, the son of Rollo, came upon them one day when he was out hunting and he rebuilt the monastery for them in 930. Most of the ruins we see today were the work of the Abbot Robert, who was at Jumièges until 1051 when he was made archbishop of Canterbury. The Church of Our Lady was consecrated the year after the conquest and despite the fact that almost all that remains of three churches that were once the pride of the Abbey is only a shell, it provides a splendid example of early Norman work. The façade, decorated with arcades, is flanked by large octagonal pillars. The transept was largely destroyed in the 19th century, but the west wall of the lantern is supported by the vast impressive sweep of a high arch.

Only the porch and the western end of the small earlier church of St Peter's are pre-Norman, built in 930; the rest of the ruins are 13th and 14th century. The remains of the 15th century chapel of St Martin and the 12th century Chapter House can still be seen and an ancient yew tree marks the centre of the former cloisters.

The monks dispersed at the time of the Revolution and the Abbey was bought for use as a stone quarry for all the farm buildings in the neighbourhood and, to facilitate this, the lantern was blown up. In 1852 a new owner undertook to preserve the remains which are now national property.

The Parish Church of Jumièges is partly 11th and 12th century but was considerably enlarged in the 16th when a few treasures and some stained glass were brought to it from the Abbey.

Beyond the diversion to Jumièges, the main road skirts the next big northward curve of the Seine, past the ferry at Duclair and runs down south where a small road leads to St Martin Boscherville.

After a superfluity of splendid ruins, the former Abbey Church of St Georges, offers the satisfying contrast of being almost intact and in its original state. It is mainly Romanesque, being built between 1080 and 1125 apart from the vaulting in the nave and transept which is 13th century. The result is an astonishing unity and simplicity of style grouped round a sturdy square tower with tapering spire.

It is designed on much the same lines as St Nicholas at Caen and has a fine Romanesque nave with 13th century vaulting and some most interesting capitals probably carved by craftsmen from Chartres.

The north face of the church which was reconstructed in the 14th century can be approached through a side door; it has fine cornice modillions and a large lantern. The 12th century Chapter house has a fine decorative frieze and is the only survival from the Abbey buildings destroyed during the revolution except for the church which was spared to be used as the Parish Church of St Martin.

St Martin de Boshcerville is only a short way from Rouen or an easy morning's drive to Dieppe.

CHAPTER X

Rouen

In this book which is devoted to a description of the Norman people and their province, I have left Rouen, their largest town until last. It is necessary to visit this lovely old city and see its interesting inhabitants in order to have a fuller understanding of this part of France. Rouen however, is not only a regional capital, it is a town which can, for the Normans, almost take the place of Paris.

Rouen has wonderful bookshops, superb churches, some museums of outstanding merit and picturesque streets that are worth exploring and are still not always too crowded to linger in. Within easy reach by train, bus or even, in summer, motorboats, there are huge forests, medieval towns and villages, splendid old abbeys and a lovely pastoral countryside as well as the whole stretch of the Seine. Then for the more adventurous, Paris is only an hour away by frequent train services, and on the other hand, Dieppe or Havre are only about thirty miles away.

At the first impact, there is a feeling that this is a busy, prosperous industrial city with ambitious new buildings such as the university as well as some excellent town planning.

Most people will be surprised to learn that Rouen is also the fourth port in France and that a large part of this development has been created since the Second World War, though a pipeline from Paris to Le Havre has decreased the number of tankers sailing up the Seine. Below the bridges of Rouen the river is lined with ships moored to wharves piled up with goods. This of course is only one aspect of Rouen which is still intellectually and socially the capital of Normandy and by far the largest town with 350,000 inhabitants. Though it suffered badly from bombardment in 1940 and 1944 when a portion of the old town lying between the Cathedral and the Seine was destroyed, an appreciable number of the old monuments have survived including more especially the superb Gothic buildings of the cathedral, and the churches of St Ouen and St Maclou. These were badly damaged but brilliantly restored for quite fortunately there were still a number of

The Woods of Normandy

fine craftsmen capable of carving stone or dealing with wrought iron.

Despite the impression of a vast new area of a modern town, within a few minutes of leaving the station, you can plunge into the old medieval city with its romantic past, its keen intellectual and artistic activities, its endless cafés and great variety of excellent restaurants where business men can enjoy first class food and the intellectuals can spend their evenings in good conversation.

The citizens of Rouen have a long tradition of sound learning and literary ability beginning perhaps with Corneille—born at 4, rue de la Pie (now a museum)— who can be regarded as the creator of the classical drama in France. Two centuries later, another Rouennais, Flaubert, who lived six miles away at Croisset, wrote *Madame Bovary* which is still considered one of the greatest novels of French literature. His pupil, Guy de Maupassant, who lived in the Château of Miromesnil near Dieppe, is perhaps the best interpreter of peasant life in the Norman countryside. If you read one of his short stories, you have the impression that you are actually living among these country folk with their covered dogcarts, their half-timbered cottages and their pawky sense of humour. All three writers attended the Lycée Corneille, the school in the former 17th and 18th century Jesuit College which gave them a superb education, and which was also attended by André Maurois, the modern writer and historian who lived some miles out of the city.

So in Rouen there is the dualism of a large business community living next door to lawyers, university teachers, writers and artists.

Claude Monet, who was intensely interested in studying the same subject under different conditions of light and in all weathers, made a number of paintings of the same haystacks in a field in Giverny and of the poplars along the banks of the Epte. He decided, in 1892, to make exhaustive studies of the Cathedral at Rouen, so he took a room in the rue du Grand Pont, from which he had a view of the cathedral façade. It was the variations of light on the forms and textures of the building which absorbed him, but he was not satisfied with the canvases he had produced in 1892, and returned the following year to continue this theme. In all, he painted twenty canvases, and his genius reveals to us much that only a practised eye could detect in the way of changes in its majestic beauty at different seasons of the year and at different times of the day and night.

I imagine that Monet would have found renewed interest in the changing effects of light on the pathetically delapidated building surrounded by rubble at the end of the Second World War. It was

Cathedral of Notre Dame, Rouen

terribly damaged, but I was privileged to witness the first stages of its restoration which were put into force incredibly quickly, and even to climb—with great trepidation—to the top of the tower. Huge pine props helped to support sections and were under the ever-watchful eyes of experienced architects responsible for preventing further collapse. I never cease to be amazed at the restoration carried out with such skill and speed, not only of the monuments of Rouen and Caen, but of the rebuilding of whole villages and towns which I saw in 1946, some reduced to a state where only a foot or two of wall remained above the ground, and any inhabitants lived in basements and cellars or under tarpaulin.

As in most countries, one good aspect of the destruction is the fact that many great monuments were cleared of some ugly buildings which obstructed a proper view of their proportions.

The main architectural sights of Rouen include the Cathedral, the churches of St Maclou and St Ouen and of course the popular Gros-Horloge built into an archway over a crowded street, which is so well known that it needs no description save that it was once on the adjoining belfry but put in a more conspicuous place by the wish of the populace in 1525 when the arch was originally built. It has sub-sequently been restored.

The Cathedral is a most complex and ornate building of which very little of the original 11th and 12th century structure is retained. The main part of the building was erected in the 13th century after a fire in 1200 and, in the 15th century, the master builder Guillaume Pontifs built the library, the staircase to it and the clerestory to the Booksellers' Court. He died at the end of the century having completed the Tour de Beurre, the prototype for the Tower at Verneuil which I mentioned earlier as being rather more graceful. Roland le Roux, who was also responsible for the Palais de Justice, was the architect of the main door in the portal and the upper part of the lantern which had its spire added in the 19th century.

The impression of great elaboration in this flamboyant architecture is somewhat relieved by the diversity of its different parts. The huge main façade with the central 16th century entrance flanked by door-ways which are surmounted by richly decorated niches and 14th century statues, the whole being a lacework of pinnacles, finials, decorated arches and gables, the intricacy relieved by the immense, and differently designed towers: the Tour de Beurre with its profusion of decoration and its final coronet in place of a spire; the Early Gothic St Romanus Tower, rather simpler and very solid looking. The south

135

The Gros-Horloge at Rouen

136

side was, to a great extent, rebuilt after the war and still has its immensely tall iron spire. Since no buildings now stand between it and the river, it can be seen to advantage from the quayside. Unfortunately the quayside itself has been rebuilt and has lost its attractive character.

The interior of the cathedral is most impressive with the lantern rising over the transept in one great upward sweep supported on huge groups of columns. There are some remarkable 13th and 14th century stained glass windows and an 11th century Crypt, but for those who are interested in individual features of the architecture and the many monuments in the interior, it is best to buy a detailed guide.

The ancient quarter has still survived around the cathedral, and restoration has transformed some of the half-timbered dwelling houses into antique shops.

The church of St Maclou which also has some fine Norman houses close to it, is more graceful and satisfying in the unity of its design and is a fine example of the Flamboyant style. Built in the middle of the 15th century, it has an unusual, five bay porch and a central tower rising up in tiers to a modern steeple. The cloister of St Maclou is one of the few remaining examples of a medieval charnel house in France.

The former abbey church of St Ouen is an excellent example of 14th century architecture, though unfortunately the west façade was rebuilt in the 19th century. Work on the building was interrupted by the Hundred Years' War so the nave was completed in the 15th century. The square central tower above the transept is topped by a strange crown of sharp pinnacles.

The interior has a superbly proportioned nave; here and in the chancel a decorative clerestory triforium runs above the great arches where there is some fine 14th century glass.

The old abbey garden can be reached through the town hall.

The churches of St Godard and St Patrick are well known for their Renaissance stained glass windows. The fine ceilings of the beautiful Palais de Justice were destroyed by fire in 1944, but the building has been restored. The great courtyard is designed with the decoration increasing on each level so that the ground floor is relatively plain, depending on fine proportion for its effect; the next floor has much enriched ornamentation on a grander scale, the one above being a crescendo of gables, pinnacles, spires and flying buttresses.

For what is left, or has been restored of the old city in the way of civic and domestic architecture, it is best to wander on a tour of discovery although a large number of half-timbered houses with carved beams were destroyed. The Place du Vieux Marché, where Joan of Arc

Church of St. Maclou, Rouen

138

Execution site of Joan of Arc in the Old Market, Rouen

was burnt, has been considerably enlarged since the 15th century, and has a covered market, but it still keeps a considerable character and attraction. Close by is the Bourgtheroulde Mansion (pronounced Boortrood) another beautiful building by Guillaume le Roux in the late Gothic and early Renaissance style. The octagonal staircase tower is soberly plain, adjoining a gloriously decorative façade, the top windows surmounted by gables, pinnacles and spires.

The Musée des Beaux Arts consists of a museum of fine Rouen pottery showing its development through the centuries, as well as a good collection of international masterpieces of paintings and works of the French School of the 17th, 18th and 19th centuries, largely by artists connected with Normandy. The Impressionists are particularly well represented and there is also a collection of 20th century works including some by Dufy and Villon.

The Secq des Tournelles, in the former church of St Lawrence close by has an important collection of ironwork of especial interest, including door knockers and hinges, balconies and signs. A Museum, arranged in the old Visitandine Convent, contains medieval stained-glass, gold and silver work, ivories, enamels and sculpture and a collection of old carved panelling, as well as the Lillebonne Mosaic and

Merovingian and Gallo-Roman remains. The Natural History Ethnography and Pre-history Museum adjoin it.

Splendid views of the Seine, the city with all its towers and the port, can be had from the Corniche, from the Belvedere, of Bonsecours and from the terrace of the University Centre.

In this book I have tried to resist the travel writer's natural tendency to overpraise his subject. It is quite true that there are some rather dull patches of countryside in Normandy; it is also true that there are regions which appear dull at first sight and gain in beauty from growing intimacy. Much of the countryside, like the countryside of Southern England, is on a small scale, so that you can find infinite variety of scenery, architecture and tradition within the space of a very few miles. The Normans themselves vary in type and character from place to place, but they have in common the qualities of great courage, persistance and a love of learning. That is why so much of the post-war reconstruction is of such wonderful quality though here again, where there has been lack of vigilence in the planning as, for instance, in the region of the landing beaches, the result has been lamentable.

When I leave Normandy I take away with me memories of these splendid forests, these lovely ponds, these little rivers winding gently through a pastoral countryside. Then, if it is springtime, I have a vision of hundreds, or even thousands, of acres of apple trees in full bloom, of

Omaha Beach

A view of Normandy

hedgerows dazzlingly white or deep crimson with may, of fields of cowslips, of woods carpeted with bluebells or daffodils and even lilies-of-the-valley. Then, there are the forests in the autumn resplendent with their flaming foliage and the winter skies so vividly rendered by Vlaminck in exciting, almost electrically charged paintings of the more dramatic manifestations of nature.

On the coast, as we have noticed, the climate is milder, the light softer and, at times, clearer. The landscape of cliffs, of fishing ports, has been so often enhanced for us in masterpieces of paintings that it needs no further description here.

I have the impression that so many British visit Normandy because it represents to them all that is typical of France. This is not really true; Normandy is, in a sense, a separate country which could survive economically, spiritually and intellectually almost independently of the rest of the world. Of the people whose virtues I have already described, most of them are deeply conscious of their kinship with the English, and, for some inexplicable reason, this consciousness has grown rather than diminished, though of course the Normans cannot fail to remember the vigorous action of the American troops who shared with the British the great task of liberating their countryside from the German yoke.

The Normans themselves have done so much to create the beauty of their countryside, but it must be admitted also that some of their greatest virtues have been developed by living in this land which is so full of infinite variety.

INDEX